GARDENING
with
COLOUR

GARDENING
WITH
COLOUR

LANCE HATTATT

This is a Parragon Publishing Book
This edition published in 2000

Parragon Publishing
Queen Street House
4 Queen Street
Bath BA1 1HE, UK

Conceived, edited, illustrated
and produced by Robert Ditchfield Publishers

ISBN 0 7525 3471 8 (Hardback)
ISBN 0 7525 3583 8 (Paperback)

A copy of the British Library Cataloguing in Publication
Data is available from the Library.

Typeset by Action Publishing Technology Ltd, Gloucester
Colour origination by Colour Quest Graphic Services Ltd,
London E9
Printed and bound in Indonesia

Half Title: A bright late summer display of *Rudbeckia*.

Frontispiece: *Helenium* 'Moerheim Beauty' in dazzling combination with
Allium spaerocephalon.

Title Page: *Clematis viticella* 'Purpurea Plena Elegans'

Opposite: A subtle early summer combination of *Allium christophii* against a
background of purple cotinus and blue *Campanula latiloba*.

THE AIM of this book is to provide the gardener with a tool to help him or her plan colour schemes in the garden. There are two essential aspects of working with colour which must always be borne in mind:

Colour effects We respond differently to each colour and to combinations of colour. This book explains the effect of individual colours within a scheme and also shows how colours can be in harmony with each other or provide contrasts, some striking, some subtle.

Colour succession It is the aim of many gardeners to keep their gardens alive with colour throughout the year. To this end this book provides a wide range of plants through the seasons, with special sections on autumn and winter subjects.

Symbols

Where measurements are given, the first is the plant's height followed by its spread.

The following symbols are also used in this book:

○ = thrives best or only in full sun

◑ = thrives best or only in part-shade

● = succeeds in full shade

E = evergreen

Where no sun symbol and no reference to sun or shade is made in the text, it can be assumed that the plant tolerates sun or light shade.

Poisonous Plants

Many plants are poisonous and it must be assumed that no part of a plant should be eaten unless it is known that it is edible.

Contents

Right: A simple but extremely effective pastel combination for early summer – pale purple dictamnus set against *Rosa* 'Iceberg'.

GARDENING WITH COLOUR

The arrangement of colour in the garden has to be one of the most satisfying and pleasurable of all the aspects of gardening. It is in this area, more than most, that the gardener is able to find real expression, working with plants to create a living picture which will not only be aesthetically pleasing to others but which will be a fulfilment of a very personal, and often frustrating, striving. For unlike the painter who controls the colours of the palette, the gardener must for ever be subject to the variables of the weather, the caprice of the seasons and the complexity of the plants themselves. But it is in these very challenges that the thrill and excitement of working with colour are to be found.

WHY COLOUR MATTERS

In the routine, day to day work of the garden it is very easy to overlook the importance of colour. So much time outdoors seems to be taken up with the seasonal tasks of endless weeding, pruning, deadheading, cutting grass, trimming edges, potting on, and similar mundane chores, that the placing of plants with regard to the maximum effect takes on a secondary role. If this is allowed to happen at all times, then one of the principal joys of the garden will be lost. Each one of us in visiting a garden, or in looking critically at our own, is aware first and foremost of the ways in which colour is used to heighten, complement or add to the design.

Gardeners, like artists, have always had a deep interest in colour and its effect in a garden setting. From the development of the great landscape parks of the past, through the preoccupation of the Victorians for colourful bedding schemes to more recent times, it is this element of gardening which, allowing for fashion, has continued to dominate. But possibly the real advances have been made during our own century. Gardeners like Gertrude Jekyll who made public her own innovative ideas on the use of colour in books like 'Colour in the Flower Garden' as well as articles such as 'Colour Effects in the Late Summer Border', have done much to influence the way in which we now think about these matters. Similarly the concept of the colour enclosure, the most famous of which is the white garden at Sissinghurst Castle created by Vita Sackville-West in the immediate post-war years, is something which has become firmly rooted in gardening tradition. Looking ahead to the future we see the highly original and bold use of colour arranged in massive drifts of a single plant currently being undertaken in a number of European countries as well as in America.

Broad sweeps of colour are used here to create impact in this summer-flowering herbaceous border.

COLOUR EFFECTS

Planning colour in any garden is something which is totally individual, a matter of personal taste. Sometimes it is the work of a single person, more often than not it is a shared occupation. Always it is a case of one preference over another.

White gardens, or white borders, have, rather sadly, been over-done, resulting in a plethora of pale imitations of those which are generally regarded as being among the best. Now perhaps is the time to move on, to experiment with more original combinations where white, whilst remaining the dominant colour, is used to contrast or to highlight other shades. For example, those who seek the reassurance of a cool, restful scheme may like to try marrying white with grey and silver. To this could be added, if desired, some of the cool blues. White with lemon, or a stronger gold, works well as does white against green. Whatever, there is room for movement

Drifts of blue forget-me-nots and yellow poppies (*Meconopsis cambrica*) have been allowed to seed at will through this carefully planned, colour themed border.

White is the dominant colour in this springtime planting.

away from the tried and tested schemes of the past towards something new, exciting and different.

Green is very much the colour of formality. Tightly clipped yew hedges, neatly arranged box-lined paths, topiary shapes together with carefully formulated foliage effects are all to be found in formal situations. Exceedingly small gardens, such as those to be had in larger towns and cities, lend themselves particularly well to this kind of treatment. Generally speaking, the smaller the area the more restricted should be the use of colour if a co-ordinated, harmonious effect is to be achieved.

The manner in which colour is used does not, very obviously, have to be limited to more traditional beds and borders. Where space is not a problem, then generous schemes may be devised for certain times of the year. These could be as simple as drifts of spring bulbs, planted in grass and allowed over the years to naturalize.

Here box is used not only to edge the border but also, clipped as a ball, to provide a note of formality.

Brick paths, lined with box, are marked at crossing points with neatly shaped domes.

Late summer and this splendid herbaceous border remains full of colour. Much of its success lies in the use of bold clumps of a single plant which are repeated at intervals.

Or, for summer colour, swathes of martagon lilies left to self-seed on the edge of a woodland. In autumn visually stunning leaf colour is easily obtained by planting groups of those trees known for their spectacular end-of-season foliage. In gardens which are so small as to accommodate only a number of pots or containers, then wonderfully colourful and interesting displays may be had all year with the introduction of imaginative, seasonal bedding.

Where a garden lends itself to division into outdoor rooms or enclosures, and these do not have to be of any great size, then much enjoyment may be had from creating a themed area which deliberately

sets out to convey a particular atmosphere or mood. Colours for something along these lines will be very much a matter of individual taste, although some consideration should be given to what lies within the immediate surroundings. It would, of course, be a mistake to devise some scheme which upon completion would sit uneasily in its environment. Purples, mauves and blacks may be employed very successfully for a sombre, even melancholy effect, if that is what appeals. Certainly there are to be found some thought-provoking, Gothic gardens which make extensive use of these colours. On a brighter note, late summer herbaceous perennials may be gathered together into a hot garden, of strong reds and yellows, which will themselves suggest climates far removed from our own.

It would be totally wrong to indicate that success, or pleasing results, may only be had where shades of a single colour, or colours which work in harmony together, are used. There are many for whom massed floral displays, such as are to be found in public parks or, indeed, to decorate road schemes in urban areas, are a constant source of delight for their very brightness and cheerfulness. There is nothing at all wrong with using colour in this manner, although it has to be said that when applied to a domestic situation, then unless great care is taken the results can appear restless and confusing. This more relaxed approach to colour is very often inevitable for those whose first love in gardening is in the forming of plant collections. In such instances the priority is usually given to the acquiring of different species and hybrids rather than the ways in which they are grouped for show of colour.

GARDENING WITH COLOUR

Very often it may prove necessary to alter the garden physically in order to execute a planned colour scheme. This may be as little as changing the shape of a border or constructing or planting a new division to form a background. On the other hand it may be far more radical like disposing of some existing feature to bring about a complete change to accommodate some new found interest. Changes of these kinds should never be a source of worry to the gardener for they are, in reality, the very essence of gardening.

Roses and clematis work happily together as companion plants to clothe the timber supports of this pergola.

Some plants, and thus some colour effects, demand certain treatment. For those who carry a love for alpines, then it is first hand knowledge that these little jewels would be lost if left to their own devices in the main borders. To be really effective, and to give of their best, they need to be placed in such a way as to resemble as closely as possible their natural habitat. Devising such a situation, and then arranging them in pleasing colour groups to extend over as long a season as possible, is but just one of the ways in which colour is used in a practical manner. Roses, possibly more than any other shrubs, lend themselves to being grouped together. The continued popularity of the rose garden is evidence of this. Sadly, all too often, these gardens turn out to be little more than a nightmare of clashing colours where little, if any, thought has been given to the overall effect. This is such a pity for roses are ideal candidates to be partnered with all manner of wonderful complementary plantings.

Not many of us are fortunate enough to possess a wood. But for those who do have some kind of woodland, even if it is no more than the shade case by a small cluster of trees, then the possibilities are almost endless. Contrary to what is generally believed, many many plants survive and thrive in shady situations. In early spring, when the canopy of leaves is down, early flowering treasures, such as the winter aconites, wild daffodils and primroses, could all be employed to provide a succession of colour based on a particular theme. Later the scheme could be varied, not only to maintain interest but to allow for later flowering shrubs and perennials.

A sunny site, which may not in itself be very large, could provide a splendid position in which to establish a tapestry carpet of thyme. These low-growing, perennial herbs, flowering over a long period, may be planted out, rather in the manner of a needlework picture, to satisfy with a rich array of colour. Depending on the plants chosen, the effect may be one of bright modernity or of faded antique. Full sun, and some shelter, may be the right conditions for growing many of the highly desirable, slightly tender perennials which are so much admired. These, in absolutely lovely colours, would be the basis for a most unusual and appealing arrangement.

Complementary roses and the sulphur-yellow foxglove (*Digitalis lutea*) provide a skilfully arranged display of colour at the start of summer.

SEASONAL COLOUR

Each one of the four seasons, around which all gardening revolves, dictates to a certain extent its own colours. Springtime suggests in the main yellow, from the palest of lemons to the deepest of buttery shades. Most likely this is on account of the primroses of the hedgerow and the wealth of cheery daffodils which contribute so much pleasure in town and country gardens alike. But it is also the colour of catkins, of witch hazels and, of course, of the flowers of the forsythia, a shrub which remains as popular as ever. As spring moves into summer, so pastel shades come into their own. Lilacs and roses, irises, campanulas, pale forms of oriental poppy, hardy cranesbill, alliums, lupins and delphiniums, the list is almost endless. Later it is the hot

Against a plain backdrop of darkly coloured foliage these flowers of flaming reds, oranges and yellows positively glow in the sunshine filtered through the leaves of a woodland area.

colours which seem to dominate, maybe in preparation for autumn which lies just around the corner.

As the year draws to a close so splendid autumnal foliage trails a blaze of fire throughout the countryside. Burnished leaves drifting through borders and piling into windswept corners possess their own particular charm. And whilst all of this, sadly, heralds the year's end, it is, not least because of the spectacular colour, both thrilling and exciting. Winter is not without considerable colour interest. Evergreens make a particularly valuable contribution for it is now, free of other border distractions, that they make their mark most clearly on the landscape. Deciduous trees and shrubs do not deserve to be overlooked. Bare branches and stems, etched against a winter sky, can look breath-takingly wonderful, particularly when dusted with hoar frost. Even the dying leaves of spent perennials add character to the garden in winter.

What all of this confirms is that colour abounds. It is for the practised gardener to decide in what ways to utilize this and to what degree. It may be a simple, seasonal approach, it may be the creation of a single colour border or it may be a totally comprehensive plan which takes in a complete garden area if not an entire garden. The important point is that the arrangement of colour in the garden, considered by many to be an art form, is not seen in isolation but rather as an exciting, integral part of the whole pattern of gardening enjoyed by so many for so much of the time.

The Colour Wheel

Traditionally the colour wheel is made up of three primary colours, red, yellow and blue. By combining these together in equal quantity binary colours, or orange, green and violet, are produced to give those pure colours to be found in the rainbow. From mixing one or more of these, in varying proportions, all other colours are obtained. Colours on the wheel, as illustrated, divide into warm and cool areas. On the warm, or hot, side are red, orange and yellow, although it has to be admitted that lemon yellows cannot be considered hot. The remaining three colours, green, blue and violet, fall onto the cool side. In a garden hot colours will advance, seeming nearer, whilst cool ones will effectively recede, appearing to be further away.

This mix of colour to be found in spring flowering tulips and wallflowers very much belongs on the hot side of the colour wheel.

Blue and violet, seen here with a touch of palest lemon, are to be found amongst the cool colours.

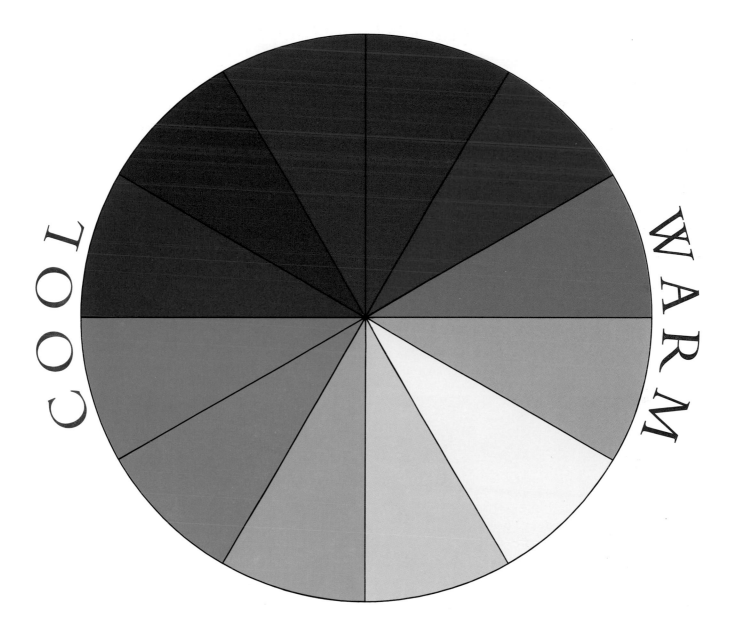

From looking at the colour wheel a number of simple points may be observed. Those colours which are positioned next to each other and which have a pigment in common are said to be in harmony. These are combinations of two or more colours which are pleasing to the eye, which do not clash and which do not strike a harsh note. For example, red and orange, yellow and green, blue and violet, these all harmonize together. Colours which appear opposite to each other on the colour wheel, often known as complementary colours, work together too. Red and green, yellow and violet, blue and orange will all complement each other although sometimes the contrast is not to everyone's taste. In any case, as a general rule, those colours which do not go together, or which do not appeal on an individual level, may be separated one from the other with the addition of white or grey.

A strong contrast is made in this springtime arrangement of Universal pansies and tulips.

Deep purple foliage becomes a perfect foil to these various shades of yellow.

Spires of yellow ligularia are set against a background of soft pink in this unusual and dramatic planting scheme.

Two unusual plants, *Isoplexis sceptrum* and *Verbascum* 'Helen Johnson', are used to great effect in this early summer border.

Pink and blue never fails to delight. Here *Clematis montana* 'Tetrarose' weaves its way through *Ceanothus* 'Puget Blue'.

The main disadvantage of the colour wheel is, of course, that it does not take into account all the varying tints, shades and hues to be found in the garden. Flowers are, understandably, much more subtle in colour than the pigments that make up the artist's palette. There are few violet flowers, and fewer red ones, when compared with the vast array of pink ones, and yet pink does not feature at all on this colour wheel. Flower colour too may be considerably altered by the shape of the actual bloom as well as by texture, so that a mop-headed blossom is likely to deepen a shade whilst an ethereal, airy one will have the opposite effect. However, colour is all about individual taste and there are not, nor should there be, any hard and fast rules.

Why Colour Varies

Unlike a painter who is able to reproduce colour exactly, the gardener is seldom, if ever, able to be so precise. Colour in nature is subject to so very many forces beyond the control of the individual that at times it would appear as if all success is a matter of chance. Of course this is not so, nor can it be. What the gardener has to do is to acknowledge these variables and to work with them, turning any disadvantage to advantage.

Most difficult to combat is the effect of the weather. Brilliant hot sunshine can alter the appearance of colour in the garden just as much as intense cold or strong winds. Rain is by no means a neutral agent. The soft, refreshing showers of early spring serve, particularly when linked to warm sunlight, to heighten and intensify colours. This in direct contrast to autumnal days of solid rain when everything, seen under lowering, grey skies, becomes almost monochromatic.

Light levels alter as the seasons change.

Bold plantings of the kind shown here cannot fail but to make an impact. *Kniphofia* 'Sunningdale Yellow' brings a brilliance to a summer border.

Pink and white astilbes are thrown into relief by their fresh green, finely cut foliage.

The white of this gladiolus is all the more startling when set against the plummy flower heads of *Sedum* 'Autumn Joy'.

Massed together these fuchsias, the flowers of which are all within the same tones, contribute colour for the greater part of the summer.

A cool, restful scene in which a white rose fans out over a generous drift of pink alstroemeria.

These in turn bring about alterations in the colour of leaves and flowers. Even within a single day it is possible to be aware of most noticeable differences in colour in the same garden when observed at different times. The pH factor of the soil, that is to say the degree to which it is acid or alkaline, will also affect colour tone as will the colour instability to be found inherent in all plants.

The best possible means by which to counter all of these things is to be confident in plant knowledge. The experienced gardener will be sure of the habits, likes and dislikes of his or her plants. The beginner will be enthusiastic and quick to learn. Both will, through trial and error, without doubt bring about the kind of successes which are to be found and enjoyed in gardens everywhere.

Winter colour, provided here with cyclamen and autumn crocuses, is all the more welcome as skies are so often cold and grey.

Delphiniums soar over other plants in a great statement of summer colour. These, of true blue, make a wonderful show.

All of these soft colours of the early summer are in complete harmony. The deep red of the astrantia (bottom left) lifts the planting and prevents it from becoming too uniform.

A midsummer border where the colours are, in the main, muted. A wine-flowered penstemon is well chosen for the way in which it draws the eye.

Using Colour in the Garden

Few would deny that one of the principal concerns of gardening is the way in which colour is employed throughout the garden. What is perhaps less immediately obvious, and certainly open to debate, are the ways and means by which gardeners consciously utilize colour in order to achieve particular effects. These may in themselves be intentionally restful schemes or ones deliberately intended to startle, if not shock. What is certain is that they in no small measure serve to give a garden individuality, making each the personal creation of its owner.

In thinking about colour in the garden it is possibly helpful to consider the extent to which it is to become an integral part of all planning. Is a particular colour border to be made in isolation, as a casual element within the garden, or is it to be planned as the main focus of a specific area? Is such a border to be viewed from all sides, as is the case with an island bed, or is it to be seen from one, or maybe two, angles only? Does the design allow for it to stand alone, or

In this garden the emphasis is clearly on summer colour. Extensive use is made of bedding plants to give this right up until the first frosts of winter.

In the right setting trees give as much impact of colour as a more traditional border.

Gold and purple are a tried and tested combination achieved here with two different berberis.

Utterly restrained and totally charming. Imaginative planting of this severity is undoubtedly helped by the formality of the surroundings.

The skill of the artist is so obviously at work in this colour grouping. Reinforced is the wisdom of using large quantities of a single plant.

Gardens need not be a riot of colour. This informally planted area relies mainly for its effect on green and acid yellow.

Quiet colours convey a sense of peace and well being. This is very much in evidence in this carefully planned border.

Packed with alpines, this simple trough is a mass of spring colour. Note the use of grit to improve drainage.

Window boxes burgeoning with colourful bedding plants are one of the traditional sights of summer. This display will remain looking good well into autumn.

These sweet peas, 'Bouquet Salmon', grown up a wigwam, form a colourful centrepiece to this mixed flower border.

should it become paired? If not an island bed, then what is to form the background? All of these are questions which will need to be addressed before thoughts and ideas are finalized and work begins in earnest.

The colour scheme or colour combinations having been fixed, decisions will need to be made about the range of plants to be included. For a border, or whole garden for that matter, which is intended to be of interest over a prolonged period, then a mixture of trees, shrubs, perennials, annuals and bulbs will probably be required. Where the effect is intended to be more seasonal, then a limited range of plants may achieve an equally satisfactory result.

In positioning colours within the garden some account should be taken of external factors. The immediate surroundings are important for they will to a large extent determine how colours will appear. Boundaries, forming a background, will need to be in harmony with colours in adjacent borders. The brick of a house, or the paintwork around the windows, may well become determining influences in deciding what should be placed where. In an enclosed area, particularly where a single colour is to be used, what is viewed before and after may have a significant bearing on what plantings are chosen. Likewise, light will play a role. White, at its best in the evening, will possess much greater luminosity in partial shade, whereas in full sunlight it will appear lack-lustre. On the other hand, blue and purple rapidly fade in the twilight. Experimentation, a major part of the fun of gardening, will lead to what is appropriate and effective in each particular situation.

Colours of the Spectrum

The following pages provide a selection of flowers and plants divided into colour groups to help you plan colour schemes. Within each colour section, plants are listed chronologically from spring to autumn/winter.

Yellow and Cream

The arrival of the daffodils in springtime is proof indeed that the gardening year is once again under way. These cheerful flowers, tossing their golden trumpets in the wind, serve as a reminder, if one were needed, that the dark days of winter are now a thing of the past. Yellow and cream are for many the colours of spring, and these shades are certainly not confined to members of the narcissus family. Flowering shrubs, like the familiar and much planted forsythia, or the less well known Chinese witch hazel, *Hamamelis* × *intermedia* 'Pallida', glow in the early sunlight. Primroses, cowslips and oxslips line the bottom of hedgerows, whilst in the garden cultivated celandines, old-fashioned leopard's bane (*Doronicum columnae*), and egg-yolk yellow alyssum flourish in the borders. Around the pond the yellow spathes of *Lysichiton americanus* add a sense of drama, rising above and over ground-hugging marsh marigolds.

But, of course, yellow and cream do not belong to a single season. Whether through flower or on account of foliage used to lighten some gloomy corner, these are shades to enjoy all year long. However, what is true, and is possibly one of the reasons why pure yellow, as opposed to cream, remains somewhat unfashionable as a colour, is that it is not always the easiest colour to place. Yellow is, without doubt, obtrusive. At all times it cries out for attention, seemingly advancing from its home in the border to meet and hold the eye. For this very reason it needs to be used with care lest it should upstage its companion plantings. Partially concealed from immediate view, to be happened upon as if by chance, a yellow border, or even a single golden foliaged shrub, may be relied upon to bring gaiety, movement and life to the dreariest of garden areas.

Hamamelis × *intermedia* **'Pallida'** Winter-flowering shrubs are always welcome during long, dark days. Although the Chinese witch hazel is slow growing, its spidery flowers more than earn a place for it in the garden. 5 × 6m/16 × 20ft

Narcissus bulbocodium Tiny though these early daffodils are, when bulbs are massed they reward with a splash of warm gold in the late winter and early spring. Plant deeply to enjoy them for many years. ○, 15 × 20cm/6 × 8in

Primula veris Cowslip are natives of the countryside and are to be found in damp meadows, hedgerows and glades. Equally at home in the garden, they may be used to brighten a spring border with their long lasting flowers. 20cm/8in

Cowslips are easily raised from seed. If dead flowerheads are not removed, then the parent plant will in time be surrounded by many little seedlings. Allow to establish before transplanting.

Primula auricula Pale lemon flowers cover this rockery primula each spring. Best grown, as here, in a position where the roots may enjoy well drained conditions. The edges of the leaves are attractively serrated and fleshy in appearance. 15 × 20cm/6 × 8in

Narcissus 'Hawera' An exciting, small flowered daffodil for springtime. It is probably true of all bulbs, and certainly of daffodils, that they are best massed together, one of a kind. Allow to naturalize over a period of years. 45cm/1.5ft

Caltha palustris Marsh marigolds contribute bold colour in spring to any area of the garden where the soil remains damp. Ideally this perennial should be planted at the margins of a pond, perhaps as an edging, or in the bog garden. ○, 30 × 45cm/1 × 1.5ft

Paeonia mlokosewitschii A strangely named, spring-flowering perennial which is well worth seeking out for its bluish-green foliage and glorious, lemony flowers which may be up to 15cm/6in across. Cultivate in humus-rich soil. 75 × 75cm/2.5 × 2.5ft

Meconopsis cambrica, the Welsh poppy, and *Euphorbia polychroma* are placed together at the base of shrubs in this colourful spring scene. The poppies will, if permitted, seed themselves freely throughout a border, and beyond, to give a casual, relaxed feel to the garden. If routine dead-heading is carried out, then it is possible to have *Meconopsis cambrica* in flower from the mid-spring through until midsummer.

***Kerria japonica* 'Pleniflora'** A vigorous shrub for spring producing a mass of double, deep yellow flowers over fresh green foliage for many weeks. Suckers, which form around the base, should be removed in order to contain the plant. 2 × 2m/6 × 6ft

***Rosa xanthina* 'Canary Bird'** Of all the shrub roses this is one of the earliest to flower when canary-yellow blooms are borne in profusion over attractive, ferny leaves. Late summer will see a second flowering. 2.2 × 2.2m/7 × 7ft

***Erythronium* 'Citronella'** An oustandingly lovely dog's tooth violet, so named on account of the shape of the spring-flowering bulb, of the very palest cream with just a hint of deeper yellow. For well drained soil in a partially shaded situation. ◖, 30 × 20cm/1ft × 8in

Rosa **'Frühlingsgold'** Butter-yellow, sweetly perfumed flowers clothe long, arching stems on this shrub rose during the late spring and the early summer. The rather lax habit fits in well with informal plantings. 2.2 × 2m/7 × 6ft

Winter pruning should be restricted to the removal of any dead or diseased wood and the thinning out of branches to maintain a clear, open middle.

Laburnum × *watereri* **'Vossii'** Grow laburnum either as a specimen tree or trained over an arch or pergola to enjoy each late spring these long racemes of seasonal colour. Be careful – all parts are poisonous. 10 × 10m/33 × 33ft

Paeonia delavayi **var. ludlowii** Tree peonies are striking shrubs to include in any border scheme. After late spring flowering, they continue to provide form and structure. This one is of deep yellow. 2.4 × 2.4/8 × 8ft

Rhodiola rosea (*Sedum rhodiola*) Glaucous leaves extend outwards to carry bracts of lime-yellow which, in bud, are distinctly tinted pink. This is a perennial for well drained soil in a position where it will enjoy full sun.
20 × 30cm/8in × 1ft

Thermopsis montana As summer approaches so this rather unusual, lupin-like perennial begins to flower. A spreading habit is such that it should be afforded plenty of space although running roots are not difficult to remove.
75 × 75cm/2.5 × 2.5ft

Early summer and this closely planted border of cream, yellow and white is alive with colour and interest. At this time of the year generous clumps of stately lupins dominate, supported with butter-yellow irises. In the foreground a white achillea catches the eye.

As may be seen, this is a border arranged to provide flower colour for the greater part of the season. To this end, careful planning is required initially at the planting stage.

Tanacetum (Chrysanthemum) parthenium 'Aureum' The golden-leafed feverfew, with its aromatic leaves, is a short-lived perennial which may be relied upon to seed around. Yellow centred flowers continue to bloom for weeks on end. 23 × 15cm/9 × 6in

This is a plant to use where a casual, informal look is required for it will pop up at will throughout the border. Unwanted seedlings are easily weeded out.

Centaurea macrocephala A cultivated form of knapweed which produces these strongly coloured flowers in the early part of the summer. Buds, of parchment brown, giving the appearance of dried paper, are most intriguing when tightly closed. 1m × 60cm/3 × 2ft

Cephalaria gigantea Primrose yellow, scabious-like flowers supported on tall growing stems first appear at the start of summer. This good-natured perennial is rarely seen in gardens and yet is easy in cultivation and may be raised readily from seed. 2 × 1.2m/6 × 4ft

Rosa **'Graham Thomas'** Certainly amongst the most free flowering of all the so named new English roses. Although the main rose time is, of course, early summer, 'Graham Thomas' will continue to bloom for the entire season and well into winter if the weather remains mild. 1.5 × 1.5m/ 5 × 5ft

To keep the growth of this shrub rose reasonably compact, prune long stems at the start of winter, to reduce wind rock, and then for a second time in the very early spring.

***Lilium* 'Mont Blanc'** Summer-flowering lilies prefer their bulbs to be placed in free draining soil. For this reason they are ideal for pot cultivation although they will succeed in the open ground. 1.2–2m/4–6ft

White flowers like these, with a mere hint of cream, would be most elegant as part of a cream/yellow scheme. If grown in pots, they could be positioned for the flowering period and then removed.

Inula magnifica An herbaceous perennial for the late summer. Placed at the back of the border these deep yellow flowers, made up of finely cut petals, are bound to make an impact, particularly where space allows for several clumps together. 2 × 1m/6 × 3ft

Tall growing plants in the main require some form of staking if they are not to collapse in strong winds. This job is best carried out in the early part of the year when new growth emerges.

***Santolina chamaecyparissus* 'Lemon Queen'** A low growing, summer-flowering shrub with grey, aromatic leaves and soft, lemon flowers. Cut back hard in the spring to retain the shape and to encourage new foliage. ○, E, 75cm × 1m/2.5 × 3ft

Santolina makes an attractive, and slightly different, edging to a path. Alternatively, it may be clipped to shape when it looks particularly effective grown as a series of balls, especially when the flowers are removed.

Brassy lysimachia, toning roses and swathes of golden rod, shortly to flower, are the principal components of this yellow scheme intended to provide colour from midsummer through into autumn.

***Kniphofia* 'Little Maid'** Pokers come into their own as the year progresses. This summer-flowering one possesses spikes of creamy yellow which are in marked contrast to the more usual hot colours. Perennial, but delay cutting back until the spring. 60 × 45cm/2 × 1.5ft

Potentilla fruticosa Shrubby potentillas are in flower for the entire summer and often well into autumn. Over winter their bare stems, of deepest brown, have a particular appeal. Little, if any, pruning is required. 1.2 × 1.2m/ 4 × 4ft

Genista aetnensis Midsummer and the Mount Etna broom is massed with sunny yellow flowers. This is a shrub to include at the back of the border where its summer colours will shine through. 4 × 4m/13 × 13ft

***Oenothera* 'Fireworks'** The brilliance of the flowers of this summer perennial are not easily ignored. This is a front of border plant for a situation where a positive and noticeable colour is needed. In flower for an extended period. ○, 45 × 30cm/1.5 × 1ft

Strong yellows, as this one, need to be placed with a certain amount of thought and care. In an open situation the eye is rapidly drawn towards them.

A magnificent stand of yellow flowered *Coreopsis verticillata* partnered with the slightly tender, velvety red *Cosmos atrosanguineus*. Exciting and imaginative combinations, like this one, lift a border and give to it an unusual and additional dimension.

Another, highly desirable coreopsis is of the palest of lemons and aptly named *Coreopsis verticillata* 'Moonbeam'. This looks wonderful in association with other perennials of mid-blue. Plant in a sunny spot.

Dahlia All of the dahlias prove themselves time and time again when late summer colour is the order of the day. This yellow pompon will continue to flower until the first of the frosts. Tubers are, of course, not hardy so should be dried off and stored over winter. From 30cm/1ft

Helianthus 'Monarch' Tall growing perennials to flower at the end of summer and which, in their colour, anticipate the onset of autumn. Plants growing to this height will always require some form of support. ◯, 2.1 × 1m/7 × 3ft

Helenium 'Golden Youth' Perennials, like this one, add warmth and colour to borders as the days of summer shorten and another season approaches. Divisions, carried out every three or so years, will guarantee free flowering plants. ◯, 1m × 60cm/3 × 2ft

Late colour is something to be planned for. All too often gardens reach a peak in the spring and early summer only to fall away as the year advances.

Helianthus 'Lemon Queen' Washed out yellows, such as the colouring of this particular helianthus, are most useful for introducing as a highlight into all manner of colour schemes. All of these daisy-type perennials come into their own in late summer. ○, 2.1 × 1m/7 × 3ft

Oenothera missouriensis A trailing form of the perennial evening primrose which is ideal either for the rock garden or to be placed at the front of the border. In flower for the greater part of the summer. 20 × 60cm/8in × 2ft

Rudbeckia fulgida 'Goldsturm' Autumn colour is captured in this late-flowering perennial which, in most garden situations, will continue to bloom for weeks on end. The principal advantage of this daisy is that it requires no staking. ○, 75 × 45cm/2.5 × 1.5ft

Gold of this kind can in some circumstances appear a little harsh. It may well prove necessary to tone down the effect with the introduction of a second, complementary colour.

Euonymus fortunei 'Emerald 'n' Gold' Variegation of the kind to be found on this small, cheerful shrub is effective throughout the year. As the weather becomes colder, so the leaves are tinged bronzy-pink. E, 1 × 1m/3 × 3ft

Ilex aquifolium 'Golden Queen' Possibly the most brilliant of all the yellow variegated cultivars of common holly. Use to lighten up any massed planting where the effect is of dull green. Strangely, despite its name, this is a male variety. E, 4 × 3m/13 × 10ft

Elaeagnus pungens 'Dicksonii' For many years the popularity of this versatile shrub has remained unchanged. Evergreen, it is most useful for providing an accent of year-round colour. Cut out any stems showing a tendency to revert. ○, E, 2.4 × 3m/8 × 10ft

Choisya ternata 'Sundance' Deep, lemon–yellow foliage characterizes this evergreen shrub which carries small, perfumed white flowers in the spring and again, to a lesser degree, in the autumn. Branches are inclined to be brittle and will snap readily under the weight of snow. ○, E, 2 × 2m/6 × 6ft

Mahonia lomariifolia Wonderfully scented flowers in late autumn and early winter are an added bonus with this distinguished, evergreen shrub. Not totally hardy, it must be given the protection of a sunny wall. E, 3 × 2m/ 10 × 6ft

All the mahonias represent good value for they are normally unfussy about both soil and situation. In flower for a considerable time.

CONSIDER ALSO:

SHRUBS:
Fremontodendron californicum (summer)
Rhododendron luteum (late spring)

ANNUALS:
Bidens 'Golden Goddess'
Calendula (marigold)
Hibiscus trionum
Tithonia 'Yellow Torch'

PERENNIALS:
Digitalis lutea (summer)
Hemerocallis lilio-asphodelus (summer)
Kirengeshoma palmata (late summer/autumn)
Primula florindae (summer)

BULBS:
Crocus chrysanthus 'Cream Beauty' (spring)
Fritillaria imperialis 'Maxima Lutea' (spring)
Iris 'Pogo' (late spring)
Tulipa 'West Point' (late spring)

CLIMBERS:
Clematis orientalis 'Bill Mackenzie' (late summer)
Hedera helix 'Buttercup' (golden foliage)
Rosa 'Mermaid' (summer)

Jasminum nudiflorum Winter jasmine is a most obliging shrub which may be trained against walls, fences or allowed to scramble down a bank. Of greatest pleasure are the flowers which appear over winter. 2.4m/8ft

Orange

Poor orange, until recently a much despised colour among gardeners. Largely uncompromising in colour, even raw, fierce to the eye and difficult to position with any certainty of success, this is a shade which has for a long time been relegated to the bottom of the heap. Yet this need not be so. For in banishing orange from a place in the border, there is a danger of ruling out of the garden many very worthy subjects. For here are to be found many of the oriental poppies, crown imperials, perennial and annual wallflowers, day lilies, traditional marigolds, moisture-loving primulas, not to mention torch-like pokers, fiery crocosmias and the bare, winter stems of the dogwood, *Salix alba vitellina* 'Britzensis'.

No, in today's climate where hot borders, the hotter the better, are not only acceptable but increasingly fashionable, orange is making a come-back. For the spirited, there is a case for clashing colours where one brilliant, vibrant shade is set against another. For those who are not wholly convinced, whose judgement is a little more reserved, then use orange more sparingly, toning it down where appropriate or limiting its use to the occasional deliberately shocking highlight. But if nothing else, find a space for one of the wonderful acers, such as *Acer palmatum* 'Osakazuki', whose spectacular autumnal foliage is more than enough to set the world alight.

Geum 'Borisii' Few other flowers share the vibrancy of colour of this form of water avens. Throughout the spring, and into early summer, this perennial will be alive with a succession of orange-red blooms held over dense hummocks of coarse green foliage. This is certainly a plant for a hot, fiery scheme, the intensity of which could be added to with generous drifts of the species tulip, *Tulipa sprengeri*, which is always one of the last to flower.
45 × 45cm/1.5 × 1.5ft

Papaver orientale Oriental poppies remain among the most reliable of all spring flowering perennials. Gorgeous, papery blooms open one after another to fill the borders with an excess of brilliant colour. These, of strong orange, are but one example of countless shades. By midsummer both foliage and flowers will have completely died down. To overcome the problem of gaps left in the border, surround them with later flowering plants such as named varieties of gypsophila. 1m × 60cm/3 × 2ft

Rosa 'Schoolgirl' Dusty orange flowers of compact shape cover this manageable climbing rose during the early part of the summer. Useful for covering a small arch or pergola or, as in this garden, to train against a brick wall. 3.5m/12ft

Rosa 'Iris Webb' A splendid floribunda rose producing a mass of soft pink blooms, each one touched with pale orange, the whole resembling a random piece of faded silk. An exciting colour combination and one which is bound to excite interest. 1.2 × 1m/4 × 3ft

Rosa 'Just Joey' These open-shaped blooms of the palest of creamy oranges enlarge in size as the weather warms. Arrange this tidy rose in groups close to a sitting-out area to appreciate the fragrant scent. 75 × 60cm/2.5 × 2ft

Rosa 'Anne Harkness' Plant this healthy floribunda either singly or as an unusual and imaginative hedge. In either case it will reward with a profusion of faded gold blooms throughout the rose season. 1.2 × 1m/4 × 3ft

Rosa 'Sweet Dream' Patio and miniature roses like this one need not be confined to the border. Free-flowering, they make excellent subjects for containers where they may be positioned for summer-long colour. 'Sweet Dream' is upright in growth and produces a mass of closely clustered flowers of apricot-orange. No pruning is necessary beyond the removal of any surplus growth in the wintertime and the taking out of diseased or dead stems.

Rosa 'Brown Velvet' Rich orange-brown blooms are set off by bronze-green, new foliage making this rarely seen floribunda a flower arranger's dream. As with all small growing roses, best effects are achieved when planted in groups. 75 × 60cm/2.5 × 2ft

Rosa 'Alchymist' Midsummer sees this shrub rose, which may also be trained to climb, a mass of full, coppery-gold flowers over attractive green leaves. All roses appreciate a winter mulch of well rotted compost to promote summer blooms. 3.5 × 2.4m/12 × 8ft

Digitalis parviflora A perennial foxglove for the first part of summer bearing tall flower spikes of a wonderfully moody, orange-brown. Foxgloves tend to enjoy a situation in the garden which is partially shaded. 1m × 30cm/3 × 1ft

***Hemerocallis* 'Stafford'** Day lilies are such versatile summer-flowering perennials, being relatively unfussy about situation and providing pleasing colour over a long period of time. This one, of deep red-orange, is one of many named varieties. 1m × 30cm/3 × 1ft

***Tropaeolum tuberosum* 'Ken Aslett'** A slightly tender climber which grows each year from an underground tuber which should, in cold areas, be lifted over winter, covered in silver sand and stored in a cool but frost-free place. Flowers, which appear in the summer, are an exotic orange with flashes of deep yellow. 'Ken Aslett' looks particularly striking placed against the dark green of a yew hedge where it may be left to scramble on its own. ○, 1.5m/5ft

Crocosmia masoniorum Still affectionately known by many as montbretia, this late summer perennial is noted for its starry, vermilion-orange flowers which hang from the tips of arching stems. Easy in both sun or partial shade.
60 × 30cm/2 × 1ft

Try placing this particular colour against a background of dark purple foliage such as may be found on the leaves of *Cotinus coggygria* 'Royal Purple' or *Sambucus nigra* 'Guincho Purple'.

***Helenium* 'Feuersiegel'** End-of-season flowers which are a mix of deepest yellow, orange, copper and blood red bring warmth to a late summer border. A perennial which you will have to search nurseries and garden centres for.
1m × 60cm/3 × 2ft

***Crocosmia* 'Harlequin'** An introduction of recent years, this gaily coloured montbretia will brighten autumnal borders for many years to come. Butter-yellow flowers are streaked in shades of red and orange. 60 × 30cm/2 × 1ft

Red

Red, so often thought of as a hot colour, is not necessarily so. On its cool side are to be found cerise pinks, shades of burgundy, crimson and deep, velvety maroons. These are colours which belong to the darker, sun loving cistus, to wonderfully antique old-fashioned roses as well as to richly tinted peonies. They are reliable shades, holding their colour well in hot sunshine when many other colours pall, and which appear jewel-like as the shadows lengthen towards the end of day. They give to the garden a feeling of well-being, of tradition firmly rooted in an accessible past.

On the other hand, the vermilions and scarlets are to be found firmly among the hot reds. With their fiery brilliance they belong to late summer and autumn. Among them are startling crocosmias, bright dahlias, lobelias, exotic physalis (Chinese lanterns), as well as the rich and varied colours to be found in the dying leaves at the turn of the year. Within the border they act as accents, advancing to arrest the eye, to advertise their somewhat strident gaiety. Used sparingly, they provide emphasis, a focal point, even a touch of daring. Overdone, they become monotonous, perhaps provoking some tedium. Within a large garden they may easily be accommodated. In a smaller area they should be used wisely and with care.

Camellia japonica 'Rubescens Major' Flowering from the early spring onwards, camellias are shrubs to include in the garden for colour at the start of the year. Their glossy green foliage is attractive in its own right and forms a backdrop to other plantings. ○, E, 3 × 3m/10 × 10ft

To flourish camellias really require acidic soil although they will perform well in conditions which are neutral. Apply a mulch of well rotted compost annually.

Akebia quinata Slightly tender, the chocolate vine needs to be positioned in full sun and afforded some protection. Given the right spot it will reward with these lovely scented flowers in the spring. 9m/30ft

***Tulipa greigii* 'Red Riding Hood'** Blood-red tulips make a bold statement in the mid-spring. This variety has unusually striped leaves of a dark maroon. Bulbs should be set out in the late autumn to flower the following year. 60 × 20cm/2ft × 8in

Rhododendron kaempferi Bursting with flower in the early spring, rhododendrons, particularly where there is space to plant in generous groups, make an impact greater almost than any other shrub. These flowers of pinky-red will delight the eye for weeks on end.

All rhododendrons are best suited to acidic soil and many prefer to be grown in partial shade where they benefit from leaf-mould.

Tulips like these with their unusual colouring give extra interest to the spring garden. Bulbs are a most useful way of adding emphasis to a scheme or the means by which a certain colour may be picked out and highlighted.

***Euphorbia griffithii* 'Fireglow'** Orange-red bracts supported on stems of a similar colour make this one of the most striking of euphorbias for the early summer. As with other perennials, cut back at the year's end. 1m × 75cm/3 × 2.5ft

Paeonia arietina Raspberry red is not to everyone's taste. However, peonies are lovely perennials to have in the garden with late spring and early summer flowers of almost every hue. They enjoy a rich feed of well rotted manure or compost. 75 × 60cm/2.5 × 2ft

Rosa moyesii **'Geranium'** Early summer flowers are followed in the autumn with the most wonderful heps ensuring colour and variety over a long period. Long, arching stems require plenty of space. 2.4 × 2.2m/8 × 7ft

Acer palmatum **var.** *dissectum* **'Garnet'** Splendid leaf colour from the beginning to the end of the year. Even in winter, without leaves, the structure of this exceedingly slow growing tree is worthy of notice. 1.5 × 2.4m/5 × 8ft

Tulipa sprengeri Virtually the last of all tulips to flower, this species excites interest as late as early summer. Flame coloured blooms may be used as a preface to hot borders later in the season. Allow to set seed in situation. ○, 45cm/1.5ft

Annual poppies, like these, bring random colour to borders especially where they are left to seed around. Those which are unwanted are removed with little trouble. Perennial oriental poppies, flowering at the start of summer, contribute a brief but dazzling show.

For a spectacular show of deep blood red with black markings, grow *Papaver orientale* 'Beauty of Livermere' reaching a height of around 1m/3ft and a spread of 60cm/2ft.

***Helianthemum* 'Supreme'** In addition to this one, approaching lipstick red, the shrub rock roses are to be found in a wide range of flower colour. Summer-flowering, they thrive in sites which are hot and well drained. E, 30cm × 1m/1 × 3ft

***Lonicera* × *brownii* 'Dropmore Scarlet'** Flowers of this climber are of an unusual shade of red which is not always easy to place. It is, however, a vigorous plant and may be relied upon to cover its chosen host with midsummer colour. 7m/23ft

Clematis **'Niobe'** Velvet textured, ruby flowers of this early summer clematis are especially appealing. This is a splendid climber to grow over a shrub or up into the lower branches of a small tree as it is unfussy about situation. 3m/10ft

Use clematis, rather in the manner of soft furnishings in an interior, to provide additional colour or to draw attention to some point of interest.

Paeonia lactiflora **'Docteur H. Barnsby'** The luxurious burgundy of this peony adds a richness to the summer border. As with all these perennials, the foliage contributes form throughout the season, particularly so as new leaves emerge. 60 × 60cm/2 × 2ft

Clematis viticella **'Madame Julia Correvon'** Almost regal in colour, this climbing viticella clematis captures attention during the late summer when it may be used to bring new life to some earlier flowering shrub. 3m/10ft

Tropaeolum speciosum Midsummer and these brilliant scarlet flowers abound. Position this climber against a dark background, as here where it grows against a dark green yew hedge, and the effect is quite spectacular. 2m/6ft

Small plants are very often difficult to establish. Pot grown specimens should be as large as you are able to find. In winter the plant is totally dormant.

Rosa 'Baron Girod de l'Ain' Wonderful colour schemes
may readily be built around the old shrub roses which,
amongst herbaceous perennials, give a border much needed
structure. These blooms mix deepest crimson with shades
of pink. 1.5 × 1.2m/5 × 4ft

Rosa 'Crimson Shower' Huge trusses of flowers do,
quite literally, shower down from this rambling rose which
is ideal to train against the wall of a house. In this situation
it is teamed with a faded pink clematis (see bottom right).
6m/20ft

Rosa 'Hunter' One of the rugosa roses which would serve
very well as a dividing hedge within the garden. Indeed, it
would make an excellent background to a border planted
up in similar shades and tones. ○, 1.5 × 1.5m/5 × 5ft

Colour is not with this type of rose restricted to the
summer flowers. Autumn sees the formation of large heps,
the colour of ripe tomatoes.

Alcea Hollyhocks serve as a reminder of a past where, in theory, every cottage garden grew these tall herbaceous perennials. Named forms are available to fit with most arrangements of colour, as this red for midsummer would testify. 2m × 60cm/6 × 2ft

Fuchsia **'Dollar Princess'** Hardy, perennial fuchsias are, perhaps, somewhat under-used in the garden proper. They do, after all, as this one of purple and red, give colour from summer right into autumn. 75 × 75cm/2.5 × 2.5ft

Pelargonium **'Lord Bute'** Who could resist such a sumptuous colour as this one, to be found in the flowers of what is commonly called a summer geranium? Overwinter in a frost free greenhouse or take cuttings at the end of the season. ○, 45 × 45cm/1.5 × 1.5ft

Penstemon **'Red Knight'** Penstemons, like this one, earn a place in the summer border for they will continue in flower, particularly when deadheaded regularly, right through until the frosts. Delay cutting back these perennials until the spring. ◯, E, 75 × 45cm/2.5 × 1.5ft

Lychnis chalcedonica This particular red is not the easiest to place and yet these perennials look so good in summer when they are planted together in a mass. Separate them from other colours simply with green. 1m × 45cm/ 3 × 1.5ft

Crocosmia **'Lucifer'** As summer draws to a close all the montbretias, as they were once known, bring borders alive with a spectacular range of colours. 'Lucifer' is particularly effective and has become a popular choice, widely available. 1.2m x 30cm/4 x 1ft

Perennial crocosmias are easily divided. Dig up an established plant, carefully disentangle and separate the distinctive corms, and then pot on or replant.

Zinnia Bring a splash of bright colour to the summer borders with fiery zinnias like these. For a show like this, simply sow seed in situ in the late spring in a sunny part of the garden. Half-hardy annuals, they should reward with flower for the season. 60cm–1m/2–3ft

Zauschneria californica Trumpets of bright red in the later part of the summer earn this perennial a place in any hot border. Plant in drifts at the front where flowers may readily be appreciated. 60 × 60cm/2 × 2ft

Dahlia **'Bishop of Llandaff'** Grown from half-hardy tubers, which must be lifted over the winter, this wonderful, red flowered, dark leafed dahlia remains, understandably, a firm favourite for the end of summer and well into autumn. 1m × 60cm/3 × 2ft

If required, dahlias may be cultivated, and kept throughout the winter, in pots. These may then be sunk into the ground where they are to flower, later to be removed.

***Helenium* 'Moerheim Beauty'** Not strictly red as such, this perennial combines within a single flower mahogany, burnt sienna, traces of orange and darkest umber. On account of this it associates perfectly with so many other colours. ◐, 1m × 60cm/3 × 2ft

This is one of the late flowering perennials to bridge the gap between summer and autumn. Plant in a large group for the most vivid and spectacular effect.

Salvia splendens It has to be admitted that this tender plant, grown as an annual, is not for those who are alarmed at too much colour. It does have a place in certain bedding schemes where it can look vibrant yet appropriate. ○, 30 × 30cm/1 × 1ft

Lobelia 'Compliment' Long spikes of rich scarlet flowers distinguish this late summer perennial which, placed in full sun, should not succumb to the winter cold. If in doubt, cover the crown at the year's end with a layer of bracken or similar material. ○, 1.2m × 30cm/4 × 1ft

Tropaeolum majus This scrambling nasturtium is easily raised each year from seed and can be planted in such a way as to weave a path through and amongst other plants. Leaves and flowers may be used to decorate salads. ○, 30 × 30cm/1 × 1ft

Godetia A hardy annual to liven up the summer borders or to include in pots and containers. This particular variety, in shades of satin red and deep pink, will produce chalice-shaped flowers all season. 25–75cm/10in–2.5ft

If preferred, the seed of godetia may be bought in mixed packets where colours will include orange, salmon, pink, violet, rose and white.

Amaranthus caudatus Love-lies-bleeding is, in fact, one of the most versatile of all annuals. It is splendid in the summer border, most effective as a cut flower, and may also be grown most successfully as a pot plant. 1.2m/4ft

***Hibiscus syriacus* 'Woodbridge'** Flowers of soft rose will be displayed on this border shrub throughout the late summer. Position in full sun and remove any dead or damaged shoots in the spring. ○, 2 × 2m/6 × 6ft

***Fuchsia* 'Checkerboard'** Strawberry-red flowers, splashed with white, hang in profusion on this eye-catching fuchsia. Use within the border or display in tubs for seasonal colour. 75 × 75cm/2.5 × 2.5ft

Fuchsias are ideal to include in hanging baskets where, provided that they are not allowed to dry out, they will flower continuously.

***Sedum* 'Autumn Joy'** Fleshy, glaucous leaves form a tight mat above which rise flat heads of rose coloured flowers which remain attractive well into winter. Even when blooms are over, this perennial has an appeal, particularly when frosted. ◯, 60 × 60cm/2 × 2ft

Schizostylis coccinea A late perennial for moisture retentive soil. These dainty flowers appear at the last, almost when everything else is over, and for this reason they are rather special inhabitants of the garden. 60 × 30cm/2 × 1ft

CONSIDER ALSO:

SHRUBS:
Chaemomeles 'Crimson and Gold' (spring)
Cytisus 'Burkwoodii' (early summer)
Magnolia liliiflora 'Nigra' (later spring)
Rosa 'Scarlet Fire' (summer)

Iris sibirica 'Helen Astor' (summer)
Potentilla atrosanguinea (summer)
Primula japonica 'Miller's Crimson' (early summer)
Viola 'Ruby Queen' (summer/autumn)

ANNUALS:
Antirrhinum 'Black Prince'
Eschscholzia 'Cherry Ripe'
Linum rubrum
Papaver commutatum 'Lady Bird'

BULBS:
Anemone fulgens (spring)
Lilium 'Journey's End' (summer)
Tulipa 'Queen of Sheba' (spring)

PERENNIALS:
Astilbe 'Federsee' (summer)
Dianthus 'Gravetye Gem' (summer)
Dicentra 'Bountiful' (late spring)

CLIMBERS:
Clematis texensis 'Gravetye Beauty' (late summer)
Rosa 'Allen Chandler' (summer)

***Berberis thunbergii* 'Rose Glow'** The chief attraction of this easy-to-grow shrub is the colour of the leaves. Wine red, splashed with pink and white, they are lovely surrounded with silver-leafed plants such as *Stachys byzantina* or one of the ghostly artemisias. 1.5 × 1.5m/ 5 × 5ft

Pinks and Pastels

It is hardly surprising that dreamy, soft, gentle colours have a widespread appeal. They are the very essence of the traditional garden with its arbours of old-fashioned roses, paths lined with lavenders, sweetly scented stocks and borders brimming with old-time favourites. All of the lovely pinks, and their associated colours of lilac, pale mauve, washed out purple, rosy red and white streaked with blue, contribute to this. And not just at one time nor in one place but all through the year in each of the seasons.

In early spring, when frosts still play havoc, wonderful camellias come into their own, their dark glossy leaves showing off waxy blooms. Then, too, the daphnes are in flower, their fragrance filling the entire garden. Later the magnolias,

cherries in blossom, and early flowering clematis. By summer there are roses, with all their companion plantings, irises, pinks and mallows, lilies and lovely, tender annuals. As warm days ebb away, and autumn approaches, Japanese anemones vie with muted asters to put on a late show. Even in the harshest of winters, brave viburnums will continue to carry sweetly scented flowers.

Little wonder that these pink and pastel shades enjoy such favourable representation in gardens everywhere. But a word of caution must be sounded. Too many pinks placed too closely together can create a cloying, overpowering effect desperate for some relief. However, by carefully mixing them with some of the quieter tones true harmony may be readily achieved.

Camellia **'Galaxie'** Camellias are very much shrubs of the early spring. Planted in and around deciduous trees, where they thrive in leaf-mould in acidic or neutral soil, they positively glow with colour at a time when the garden may often seem bare. Place two or three together, and underplant with seasonal small bulbs in similar or toning shades, for an exciting start to the gardening year. ◯, E, 2 × 2m/6 × 6ft

***Camellia* 'Water Lily'** As spring moves on towards summer, and these sugar-pink blooms have long faded and become a distant memory, this shrub, on account of its glossy, evergreen leaves, will remain a distinctive feature of the border. ◯, E, 2 × 2m/6 × 6ft

***Prunus cerasifera* 'Nigra'** Myriads of tiny, single pink flowers, which will gradually fade to a pale blush, festoon this small tree in the first part of spring. Stems, and young foliage, are of blackish-purple. 4.5 × 4.5m/15 × 15ft

***Magnolia* × *soulangeana* 'Lennei'** A vigorous, spreading tree producing rose-purple, goblet-type flowers which are stained purple and creamy-white on the insides. A mature specimen is one of the sights of spring, particularly set against a clear blue sky. ◯, 3 × 3m/10 × 10ft

Clematis macropetala 'Markham's Pink' A truly delightful, early flowering climber which can be most effective when left to its own devices to weave a passage among other springtime plantings. In this garden it is teamed with the blue *Clematis macropetala* for the freshest of combinations. Both of these clematis require no more in the way of pruning than the removal of any unwanted stems in the late winter. At that time they will benefit from a good mulch at the base of the plant of well-rotted compost. 1.8m/6ft

Clematis alpina 'Willy' Seen here with a planting of the hardy cranesbill, *Geranium macrorrhizum*, this prettily flowered climber is a delight in the spring. Taking up very little in the way of space, such clematis are readily incorporated into most schemes. 2.4m/8ft

Clematis 'Nelly Moser' Flowering in the spring with large cartwheels of pale pink with a mauve-lilac bar, 'Nelly Moser' never loses popularity. A second flush of blooms is often to be had in the later part of summer. ○, 2.4m/8ft

Malus × moerlandsii **'Profusion'** Flowering crab-apples are always lovely when heavy with blossom in springtime. This one boasts slightly fragrant flowers of dark pink set off by juvenile foliage which is distinctly coppery. Later on there will be deep red fruits to enjoy. Among the crabs are to be found trees which are very suitable for even quite small gardens. Many make for fine specimens set within a lawn or grass area. 4.5 × 4.5m/15 × 15ft

Epimedium × youngianum **'Roseum'** Make a point of cutting the previous year's foliage back to ground level before the dainty spring flowers of this perennial plant emerge. As the year progresses, so new leaves will mature. 25 × 30cm/10in × 1ft

Scilla non-scripta Pink bluebells may sound rather strange, but they make a welcome change in spring from the more widely seen blue ones. Leave bulbs undisturbed to naturalize in a wooded or wild part of the garden. ◯, 25cm/10in

***Prunus tenella* 'Firehill'** Mid-pink flowers in spring extend along the length of the branches of this compact shrub. Use as a centrepiece to a small border or plant in a group, say three or five, as a statement of colour. ○, 2 × 2m/6 × 6ft

***Paeonia suffruticosa* 'Sitifukujin'** Seven Gods of Fortune is rather an appealing, romantic name for this tree peony which carries its fine flowers in the spring. Long-lived, the tree peonies contribute something a little different to the garden. ○, 2.2 × 2.2m/7 × 7ft

***Daphne* × *burkwoodii* 'Somerset'** Heavily scented, spring flowering daphnes really do have to be included if at all possible. Slow growing, they are not difficult to accommodate and will, like this one with its pale pink flowers gathered together in clusters, delight for a long period of time. Plant with hellebores, old-fashioned, double primulas, epimediums and different varieties of pulmonaria to create a spring garden full of interest and colour. To this arrangement may be added any number of bulbs. ○, Semi–E, 1.5 × 1m/5 × 3ft

***Paeonia lactiflora* 'Monsieur Jules Elie'** Possibly of all herbaceous plants, peonies give some of the greatest pleasure. Their large, slightly blowzy heads belong to the early summer where they join with irises and the first of the roses. 1 × 1m/3 × 3ft

Incarvillea delavayi From a basal rosette of tapering, pinnate leaves rise rather shocking pink flowers held at the top of short stems. This is an early summer perennial for rich soil in full sun. ◯, 60 × 30cm/2 × 1ft

***Deutzia* × *elegantissima* 'Rosealind'** Tiny flowers are massed together on this shrub which blooms from the late spring into the early summer. After the flowering time is over, use it as a host plant for a late clematis to prolong the period of colour. 1 × 1.5m/3 × 5ft

Deutzias should be hard pruned immediately after flowering. This prevents leggy stems and produces a more compact bush.

Tulipa 'China Pink' As spring moves towards summer, fill the borders with these satin-pink, lily-flowered tulips. For best results, plant bulbs deeply in the autumn with a dozen or more to each planting hole. 45cm/1.5ft

Rosa 'May Queen' Large blooms of an old rose pink appear in profusion on this rambling rose in the first part of the summer. Suitable for growing against a house or to train along a boundary fence. 5m/15ft

Primula vialii An unusual, summer-flowering perennial with cone-like flowers, scarlet in bud and which open to a lavender-pink. Plant in moisture retentive soil around the margins of a pond or at the edges of a stream. 30 × 30cm/1 × 1ft

***Rosa* 'Pink Elizabeth Arden'** Furnish large mixed borders at the start of summer with shrub roses such as this one. Their arching stems provide instant structure and can on occasion be utilized to act as supports to tall growing perennials which surround them. Group them together in single varieties where there is space, or in complementary colours where greater variety is wanted. Feed generously to promote more flowers. 1.5 × 1.5m/5 × 5ft

***Chaerophyllum hirsutum* 'Roseum'** In appearance this perennial is not at all dissimilar to a pink cow parsley but is, in fact, very much more refined. Position to flower in the late spring to give a lightness among other herbaceous plants. 60 × 60cm/2 × 2ft

***Prunella grandiflora* 'Pink Loveliness'** Spikes of pink flowers cover this low-growing perennial for many weeks in the summertime. This is a plant to carpet an area of rock garden or, in greater numbers, to act as ground cover. 30 × 30cm/1ft × 1ft

Penstemon venustus A penstemon for the early summer. Given good drainage and a sunny situation this variety should prove to be reliably hardy in the majority of gardens. Avoid cutting back until well into spring. 45 × 45cm/1.5 × 1.5ft

***Geranium cinereum* 'Ballerina'** Of all the perennial, hardy cranesbill, this one, which forms a neat plant, is utterly charming and certainly deserves to be grown. After the summer flowers the leaves remain as pretty. 20 × 30cm/ 8in × 1ft

Lathyrus grandiflorus Shades of magenta are to be found in this climbing, everlasting pea. Vigorous, it will put on enough growth in one season to cover a fence or, if trained, climb the wall of a house to decorate it with traditional sweet pea flowers. ○, 1.5m/5ft

Each autumn, or in the spring if you prefer, remove all of the old, dead foliage and cut the stems back to ground level.

***Clematis viticella* 'Margot Koster'** Rosy-pink flowers of deep hue are larger than are normally to be found on a viticella clematis. In bloom for the greater part of the summer, it is best planted where the overall effect is to be seen. 3m/10ft

Papaver rhoeas A colourful annual which is developed from the field poppy which is to be seen trailing a path of glory in summer. This variety is an exciting double form of icing-sugar pink. 45cm/1.5ft

Rosa **'Princess Marie'** Large, rambling roses, like the one pictured here, may be used to climb into trees where they will swathe them in glorious bloom in the midsummer. Once started, let them wander at will. 4.5m/15ft

Rosa **'Raubritter'** Clusters of semi-double, lilac-pink cupped flowers appear in summer over foliage which is inclined towards the grey-green. Unfortunately this rose is only slightly scented. 1 × 1.5/3 × 5ft

Rosa **'Albertine'** Salmon buds of this well known, popular rambling rose open to a copper-pink which is shown off by new leaves which are red tinted. Most suitable for growing over a pergola as in this garden. 5.4m/18ft

Oxalis articulata Enjoy these delightful mauve-pink flowers from the late spring onwards. A low growing, easily cultivated perennial which, unlike other varieties of oxalis, is not invasive. Useful as it will tolerate most situations including dry shade. 20 × 20cm/8 × 8in

For a named form, look out for *Oxalis articulata* 'Foundation Pink' which is exactly powder pink. In flower virtually all year and lovely for including in indoor posies.

Digitalis × mertonensis Perennial flowers, opening in summer, of this form of foxglove closely resemble the colour of crushed strawberries. It benefits from division every two or three years. 1m × 60cm/3 × 2ft

Phlox paniculata 'Fairy's Petticoat' Border phloxes are one of the mainstays of the summer border and will, amongst other perennials, flower for several weeks at a time. Dead-head regularly to keep plants looking good. 75 × 60cm/2.5 × 2ft

Hydrangea macrophylla As summer gathers pace, so the large mopheads of the hydrangeas come into their own. Uncompromising though the flowers may be, they do contribute most worthwhile colour to shrub borders where, as the year moves on, they will fade, and may indeed be dried, to magnificent shades of damask. Colour will always vary according to soil type. Hydrangeas are also ideal subjects for tubs or large containers. However, they must not be allowed to dry out. 2 × 2.4m/6 × 8ft

***Hydrangea macrophylla* 'Ayesha'** The lilac-pink flowers of
this particular hydrangea are unique for the way in which
the petals are curved. For best results choose a place in the
garden which is slightly shaded. 1 × 1.5m/3 × 5ft

Lythrum salicaria Purple loosestrife, as it is commonly
known, is a graceful plant which is well suited to be grown
in damp conditions in either a bog garden or at the
waterside. Easy in sun or part shade. 1m × 30cm/3 × 1ft

***Clematis texensis* 'Princess of Wales'** A late flowering
clematis carrying trumpets of deepest pink. Rather than
plant to climb, trail this one through the border for end-
of-summer colour. Hard prune in early spring. 3m/10ft

Echinacea purpurea Purple coneflowers are amongst the most striking of perennials to include in the late summer herbaceous border. Combine them, as here, with *Achillea millefolium* 'Cerise Queen'. Both make good flowers for cutting and arranging indoors. 1.2m × 60cm/4 × 2ft

***Fuchsia* 'Garden News'** All of the hardy fuchsias bring to the garden long lasting, end-of-summer colour which continues well into autumn until the first of the frosts. In very cold areas pile compost or old ferns over the crowns. 60 × 60cm/2 × 2ft

***Oenothera speciosa* 'Pink Petticoats'** A pale pink form of the evening primrose to spread gently across the ground at the front of a border. Preferring a sunny spot, it should be encouraged to drift at the base of taller growing plants throughout the summer. This is the kind of perennial over which it would be fun to train a small flowered clematis for a decorative, well furnished look. 15 × 60cm/6in × 2ft

Lobelia × ***speciosa*** hybrid Rich soil, which is not allowed to dry out, is a requirement of this summer perennial from Mexico. To this may be added leaf-mould. Various named forms may be obtained from specialist nurseries. 75 × 45cm/2.5 × 1.5ft

Lilium speciosum **var.** ***rubrum*** A wonderfully fragrant Japanese lily which, surprisingly, does not come into flower until the late summer or early autumn. This particular variety is heavily stained a rich carmine colour. Afford these lilies plenty of humus. 1.5m/5ft

Crinum × ***powellii*** An exceedingly handsome, bulbous plant sporting beautiful trumpet-shaped flowers over strap-like foliage. To succeed, these really do need to be planted in a hot position in full sun and in soil which is particularly free-draining. Ideally, such a border would be backed by a wall for added protection. However, if you have some of these conditions, then given them a go. ○, 1m × 60cm/3 × 2ft

Schizostylis coccinea **'Sunrise'** Enjoy these late flowering perennials in the autumn at a time when most other herbaceous plants are going over. Associating well with water, they are actually perfectly happy in normal garden conditions. 60 × 30cm/2 × 1ft

Gypsophila **'Rosy Veil'** All the gypsophilas, or baby's breath as they are sometimes known, are useful as summer perennials for creating a light, airy feeling among other plants. This one, which forms a low mat, has tiny white flowers tinted pink. 20 × 30cm/8in × 1ft

Nerine bowdenii These autumn flowering bulbs hail from South Africa so are, understandably, in need of a site where they may enjoy as much sunshine as possible. In this instance they are to be seen blooming with some late phlox of a similar colour tone. ○, 45 × 20cm/1.5ft × 8in

If you do not have anywhere suitable to grow them, then try them in pots which may be placed for the flowering season where they may be easily seen.

Aster novi-belgii **'Goliath'** Autumn Michaelmas daisies bring life to the garden as days begin to shorten and thoughts turn towards the passing of the year. 'Goliath', planted in a sunny situation, will reward for several weeks with these pink flowers with their bold yellow centres.

If possible, try to create an area of the garden especially devoted to autumn-flowering plants. It will help to detract from the onset of winter. ○, 1.2m × 45cm/4 × 1.5ft

Colchicum speciosum Dwarf flowering bulbs for the autumn assist in extending the season. In this arrangement colchicums are planted to poke through the leaves of a variegated vinca, or periwinkle, which acts as ground cover. ○, 20 × 20cm/8 × 8in

The large basal leaves appear after the flowers in late winter or early spring.

Cleome spinosa The spider flower, so known because of its spider-like flowers, is an annual which deserves more widespread cultivation. The rose coloured flowers, pictured here, are particularly appealing. Use it to fill any gaps in borders. 1m/3ft

Verbena **'Aveyron'** A perennial verbena for end-of-season colour. Plants like this really need to be massed together, rather in the way of bedding, to achieve a purposeful effect designed to make a statement. 60 × 30cm/2 × 1ft

Arbutus unedo f. *rubra* If you have space, and your soil is inclined towards the acidic, then do try this splendid form of the strawberry tree. Strangely, it flowers in the autumn at the same time as its fruits begin to ripen. In this picture it is possible to see a number of the unripened fruits which will redden with the passing of time. E, 5 × 5m/16 × 16ft

Physostegia virginiana The obedient plant is so named for the way in which the flower stems may be bent and will then remain in position. This late summer perennial is ideal for planting in between shrubs where it will gradually spread to form an effective and decorative form of ground cover. Once the flowers are over, the whole plant may be cut down to ground level. This is carried out either in the late autumn or early spring. 30 × 30cm/1 × 1ft

---

CONSIDER ALSO:

SHRUBS:
Cistus 'Silver Pink' (summer)
Kolkwitzia amabilis 'Pink Cloud' (summer)
Rhododendron yakushimanum (spring)
Rosa 'Dearest' (summer)
Viburbum × bodnantense 'Dawn' (autumn-winter)
Weigela florida 'Foliis Purpureis' (summer)

ANNUALS:
Cosmos 'Daydream'
Lavatera trimestris 'Pink Beauty'
Saponaria vicaria 'Alba'

PERENNIALS:
Anemone × hybrida 'Queen Charlotte' (late summer-autumn)
Astilbe 'Amethyst' (summer)
Dierama pulcherrimum

(summer)
Hemerocallis 'Catherine Woodbury' (summer)
Phlox 'Mother of Pearl' (summer-autumn)
Tradescantia × andersoniana 'Pauline' (summer)

BULBS:
Allium oreophilum (summer)
Anemone blanda 'Pink Star' (spring)
Lilium 'Pink Perfection' (summer)
Lilium tigrinum 'Pink' (summer)

CLIMBERS:
Clematis 'Comtesse de Bouchaud' (late summer)
Clematis montana 'Tetrarose' (spring)
Rosa 'Madame Caroline Testout' (summer)

Amaryllis belladonna This lovely perfumed bulb should not be confused with *Hippeastrum*, the large flowered pot plant which appears for sale around Christmas. Plant deeply in a sheltered position away from cold winds and feed in spring. ○, 75cm/2.5ft

Purple and Lilac

Of all colours, these are possibly amongst the most moody, often associated, together with black, as the colours of mourning. However, by widening the range to include some shades of lavender, magenta and the darkest of ruby reds, then some exciting variations are realized. Indeed, without them purple, placed on its own in a mass, would appear sombre, depressing and lifeless. As it is, used thoughtfully and in an imaginative manner, it opens the way to almost limitless, original combinations.

Bearing in mind the potential for creating totally deadening effects, then purple is most certainly not a colour for shade. Where possible such hues are best viewed back-lit, that is to say with the sun shining through them from behind.

When this occurs, both foliage and flower adopt a magical quality that surprises as much as it delights. If at all possible, then try to contrive such an area within a much frequented part of the garden. Whatever, avoid placing close to the boundaries of a country garden for this is a colour which does not associate well with green fields.

Although purple is as much a colour for spring, with crocuses, Pasque flowers, dark anemones and violets, as for summer with stately irises and velvety roses, it is as the year develops that it really comes into its own. Late summer and autumn bring with them dark flowered fuchsias, richly coloured asters, the lustrous berries of the calli-carpas and, by no means least, the splendid, tall-growing, airy *Verbena bonariensis*.

Crocus tommasinianus Early spring colour develops with these tiny bulbs. Left undisturbed, they will gradually increase with time. Best planted underneath a deciduous shrub or at the base of a tree where they may be forgotten once the flowering period is past. 10cm/4in

Small flowers need to be given an importance otherwise they fail to attract notice. One way of doing this is to plant in purposeful clumps or drifts.

Pulsatilla vulgaris Rich purple, spring flowers crowd together over ferny foliage on this perennial plant. The Pasque flower is suitable either for the rock garden or scree bed, or for the front of the border. 30 × 30cm/1 × 1ft

Both red and white forms may be found in nurseries and garden centres making this a plant for a number of different colour schemes. Silky seed heads appear later in the year.

Fritillaria meleagris A spring bulb which is totally at home growing in grass. Mottled purple flower heads hang from slender stems giving the snake's head fritillary a slightly sinister appearance. Allow to set seed. ○, 25cm/10in

Rhododendron augustinii A mature bush of this evergreen shrub is massed each spring with these lovely, blush-lilac flowers which crowd over the tiny leaves. Excellent for growing in light woodland. ○, E, 3 × 3m/10 × 10ft

Aquilegia vulgaris **'Adelaide Addison'** Moody violet–blue, semi-double flower heads splashed with white contribute depth to a border. Allow these spring and early summer perennials to seed around when they will produce some interesting colour combinations. ◯, 75 × 45cm/ 2.5 × 1.5ft

Nepeta mussinii All of the catmints, and this one is no exception, deserve to be widely planted as they are seldom out of place in any colour scheme. Completely hardy, cut back when the early summer flowers are over; replacements will soon follow. 45 × 75cm/1.5 × 2.5ft

Tulipa **'Blue Heron'** Flowering in the late spring, this wonderful violet-purple tulip has crystal-like fringes all around the top of the petals, rather like miniature, frosted icicles. Imagine a mass around some dark leafed shrub like the smoke bush, *Cotinus* 'Grace', or a richly coloured berberis. In planting, remember that the best effects are achieved through more of less. Stick to a single variety of bulb in one area and plant in as large a number as you can afford and for which you have the space. ◯, 60cm/2ft

Clematis 'Proteus' Blooms of a delicate mauve-pink, appearing slightly washed out, are set off by foliage of a fresh green. Although this is a climber, as are the majority of clematis, try training its stems horizontally through the border. 2m/6ft

The main flowering period for 'Proteus' is in the first part of the summer. However, it will produce a reasonable second show at the approach of autumn.

Abutilon suntense Late spring onwards sees this shrub in flower. Slightly tender, it will benefit from some wall protection in a situation where it may bask in full sun. ◐, 5 × 3m/15 × 10ft

Wisteria floribunda One of the loveliest sights of the early summer is to see the walls of a house fully clothed, as here, with the long flower racemes of a well-grown wisteria. In this instance the climber is complemented by *Ceanothus thyrsiflorus* var. *repens*. ◐, 9m/30ft

***Clematis* 'Haku-ôkan'** Distinctive, violet-purple blooms are carried on this climber towards the end of spring and at the start of summer. A second flowering takes place in the early days of autumn. Use it as a means of highlighting a particular colour theme of similar tones. 2m/6ft

Within this garden a sunny slope has been used with great imagination and artistry. Different creeping thymes, with an emphasis on dark purple, have been arranged to resemble an antique rug thrown carelessly to one side. The skill has been to limit the varieties so that the overall effect is in no way confusing. Given similar conditions of warmth and free-draining soil, then this is an idea which could easily be adapted, even on a reduced scale.

Trifolium rubens An unusual perennial which is, as it happens, a member of the clover family. From a neat clump of trefoil foliage emerge these flower heads of purplish-red in the early summer. In bud they are of a rather wispy appearance. 30 × 30cm/1 × 1ft

Malva sylvestris mauritiana Almost the colour of Victorian mourning, these rich flowers appear on this tall-growing perennial on and off from spring right through until autumn. Essential to plant in full sun. ○, 1.2m × 60cm/ 4 × 2ft

***Allium aflatunense* 'Purple Sensation'** Combine this tall-growing bulb, one of the onion family, with purple bearded irises for spectacular springtime colour and interest. Ensure bulbs are planted in light, well-drained soil. 1m/3ft

***Iris* 'Mandarin'** For sheer elegance and beauty, then this iris must come close to the top of the list. In this planting it looks particularly fine in early summer against the lime-green bracts of the euphorbia positioned behind it. 1m × 30cm/3 × 1ft

Penstemon glaber All of the penstemons, and this early summer one is no different, will repay dead-heading carried out regularly with a succession of flowers for weeks on end. Choose glaber for a scheme centred on soft mauve. To extend the season, and to strike a more positive note, select *Penstemon* 'Papal Purple', *Penstemon* 'Blackbird' and *Penstemon* 'Catherine de la Mare', all of which will be in flower from midsummer onwards. ○, E, 60 × 60cm/ 2 × 2ft

Rosa **'Zigeunerknabe'** ('Gipsy Boy') Summer-flowering roses are the very essence of any garden and are wonderful shrubs around which to centre a colour scheme. So many of the perennials of soft, pastel shades in flower at this time will complement them. 1.5 × 1.2m/5 × 4ft

Rosa **'Bleu Magenta'** Clusters of violet-crimson blooms cling to the arching stems of this climbing rose which may, as pictured here, be closely trained against a wall. 4.5m/15ft

Rosa **'Blue Boy'** Place this shrub rose as the centrepiece of a border devoted to shades of crimson, magenta, deep pink and violet for an exciting and out of the ordinary picture. Dead-head to promote more strongly scented flowers. 1 × 1m/3 × 3ft

The old idea of 'The Rose Garden' is, thankfully, no longer with us. Instead roses should be seen as versatile and adaptable shrubs to be used widely throughout the garden in all manner of situations and combinations.

Phlox **'Chattahoochee'** For spring colour in the rock garden, then plant this pale lilac, dark–centred perennial phlox in a sunny spot. Two or three placed together will form an attractive carpet to smother weeds. 20 × 30cm/ 8in × 1ft

Rosa **'Veilchenblau'** A striking, free flowering rose to climb over a pergola or to be placed against a wall or fence. Violet blooms, streaked with white, gradually fade to lilac-grey. 3.5m/12ft

Erigeron speciosus **'Pink Jewel'** This lilac-pink daisy with a centre of old gold will be in flower each year all through the summer. Use it in association with the early Michaelmas daisy, *Aster frikartii* 'Mönch', which is similar in appearance but of a different hue, and against the wine- red leaves of *Euphorbia dulcis* 'Chameleon'. Through this could be trained some clematis of complementary colour whilst any gaps could be filled with appropriate annuals. 75 × 30cm/2.5 × 1ft

Salvia sclarea* var. *turkestanica Faded lavender and purple bracts appear from the midsummer on this biennial form of sage. Left to seed around, it has a charming habit of appearing in just the right place. 75 × 30cm/2.5 × 1ft

Acanthus spinosissimus A perennial which makes a statement and presents a different, and often welcome, form. As attractive as the flowers, appearing in midsummer, are the leaves which are of a good green and are finely cut. ◐, 1.2 × 75cm/4 × 2.5ft

***Clematis viticella* 'Etoile Violette'** All of the later flowering clematis are deserving of a place in the garden and this one, with its deep purple petals and distinctive cream stamens, is surely one of the best. Flowers first appear in midsummer and continue well into autumn. 3m/10ft

Viticella clematis are hard pruned in the late winter to ground level. This makes them ideally suited to be grown through other flowering trees and shrubs for they can never become a problem.

Aster frikartii **'Mönch'** It is not difficult to find words of praise for this summer-flowering Michaelmas daisy. Free of mildew, which so often besets these perennials, it blooms for months on end, the soft lilac flowers never difficult to place. ◯, 75 × 45cm/2.5 × 1.5ft

Verbena bonariensis Grow this short-lived perennial, but one which may be relied upon to seed around the parent plant, at the front of the border to look through a sea of purple to the other good things which lie beyond. From midsummer onwards. 1.2m × 15cm/4ft × 6in

Allium sphaerocephalon Commonly known as the round-headed leek, these spherical globe flowers may be used to grow up through other summer plantings to add a further dimension. Bulbs are particularly useful for this purpose for, as these, they take up very little ground space in relation to the impact that they are able to make. Always, though, plant in sufficient numbers to look purposeful. 30–60cm/1–2ft

Passiflora caerulea The common name for this lovely summer climber is derived from the early Spanish missionaries in South America who saw in the flower instances of Christ's Passion. Of all the passion flowers, it is probably the hardiest. ○, 6m/20ft

***Geranium clarkei* 'Kashmir Purple'** All of the perennial hardy geraniums make exceedingly garden-worthy plants. This one, flowering in the summer, will be attractive either with plants of a similar colour or to act as a contrast. 30 × 30cm/1 × 1ft

This section of a late summer border brings together shrubs and perennials of similar tones but quite different colours, showing ways in which it is possible to create harmonious arrangements out of doors. Plants featuring here are *Hydrangea aspera* Villosa Group, a border phlox and the flat heads of *Achillea millefolium* 'Lilac Beauty'. Once the core of this kind of grouping has been established, then it is very easy to add to it or to expand the idea within a much larger area.

Lavenders possess an old-fashioned quality, always being associated in our minds with the cottage gardens of the past. As illustrated here, they may be planted together to join up as an informal, but colourful and scented hedge.

Brushing against this in the kitchen garden when gathering the beans would be a pleasurable experience. If cut back hard in the spring, bushes will retain their shape and not become woody.

***Buddleja davidii* 'Dartmoor'** Long, lilac flower spikes appear on the current season's growth of this shrub towards the end of summer. Like the majority of buddlejas, this one acts as a powerful magnet in attracting butterflies. 3 × 3m/10 × 10ft

Gladiolus papilio This delicately flowered gladiolus of faded lilac-pink is in flower as summer draws to a close. A perennial for the edge of the border for it needs to be seen close up to be appreciated. 1m/3ft

Salvia horminum Grow this particular form of annual clary for its dark violet bracts in summertime. An excellent plant for flower arrangers as it may be used either fresh or cut and then dried for winter use. 45cm/1.5ft

In this garden setting the clary is grown against a hardy fuchsia. Both flower colours complement each other with a richness as well as a variety of form.

Eupatorium purpureum A tall growing perennial for the end of summer. The pale pinkish-mauve flowers of the Joe-Pye weed are held on stiff stems that seldom need staking. Place in rich, moisture retentive soil in sun or part shade. 2 × 1m/6 × 3ft

Clematis viticella 'Purpurea Plena Elegans' Lovely, double blooms of deepest purple are set free among the last of the flowers of the pinky-red valerian, *Centranthus ruber*. This is a climber for late summer and early autumn. 3.5m/12ft

An autumn border at its best. Michaelmas daisies, in shades of pale mauve, lavender and lilac, are grouped together in this garden to give a dreamy, misty effect designed to instil a sense of well-being and satisfaction as the gardening year enters its final phase. To achieve this, or something similar, it is necessary to plant large clumps in bold drifts. As a general rule, the colours of all the asters look well together with the possible exception of white which can, occasionally, interrupt a flow.

CONSIDER ALSO:

SHRUBS:
Buddleja alternifolia (early summer)
Buddleja davidii 'Black Knight' (late summer)
Fuchsia 'Margaret' (late summer/autumn)
Lavandula angustifolia 'Grappenhall' (summer)
Syringa 'Elinor' (early summer)

ANNUALS:
Heliotropium 'Marine'
Lathyrus odoratus 'North Shore'
Petunia 'Plum Purple'

PERENNIALS:
Campanula glomerata 'Superba' (early summer)

Geranium magnificum (summer)
Iris chrysographes (summer)
Liriope muscari (autumn)
Origanum laevigatum (late summer/autumn)
Viola odorata 'Princess of Wales' (spring)

BULBS:
Crocus speciosus (autumn)
Iris reticulata (spring)
Tulipa 'First Lady'

CLIMBERS:
Clematis 'Jackmanii' (late summer/autumn)
Solanum crispum 'Glasnevin' (summer/autumn)
Wisteria floribunda 'Violacea Plena' (late spring)

Clematis 'Gypsy Queen' Plum–purple flowers appear on this climber from the middle of summer through until autumn. Hard prune during the wintertime. 3m/10ft

Blue

Blue remains one of the most covetable of all colours within the garden. Perhaps this is in no small measure because of its shy, retiring habit. Unassertive, it is one of the last colours to declare itself in the early morning and, as the dusk gathers, the first to fade from prominence. Because of this it is useful for creating a sense of distance, for conveying the impression that a border, or indeed garden, is actually rather longer than it in fact is.

Blue used singly may well appear a little dull, lifeless and lack-lustre. It is a colour to be partnered with others in a deliberately thought out scheme, or to be a token, a mere suggestion, within a mixed colour border. Placed among yellows, whether the soft primrose of early spring or the more strident golds of midsummer, it is immediately brought into focus and given added definition. In a different context the mistier shades of blue may be used to great effect in an alluring scheme made up of soft, pastel pinks, mauves and, more daringly, lime greens.

Lithodora diffusa Poor, stony, lime-free soil is the ideal medium in which to grow this attractive, small shrub which will produce these intense blue flowers for the greater part of the summer. A suitable candidate for the rock garden. 30 × 60cm/1 × 2ft

Lithodora is not a particularly long-lived plant. Stocks may be replenished every few years with cuttings taken in the midsummer. Set these out in a mixture of equal parts of sand and peat.

Scilla mischtschenkoana Start the year with early flowering squills. This one, rather impossibly named, is of the palest of blues and enjoys a situation which is not too hot and which is rich in humus. Leave bulbs undisturbed to naturalize. 10cm/4in

Chionodoxa luciliae Glory of the Snow is the name by which these tiny bulbs are most commonly known. The pretty blue and white flowers appear, as the name would suggest, in the later part of the winter or at the start of the spring. 10cm/4in

Clematis **'Blue Bird'** Choose early spring flowering clematis for a splash of colour at the start of the year. All of the alpina types, and 'Blue Bird' is no exception to this, look particularly effective when trained to grow through some low-growing shrub which will flower later on.

Pruning is restricted to cutting out any dead or weak stems and generally tidying the plant during the late winter. All clematis respond to an annual mulch of well rotted compost or similar material. 1.8–2.4m/6–8ft

Gentiana acaulis Such a blue as this one is almost irresistible and creates a moment of drama in the spring rock garden. Perennial gentians prefer a soil which is inclined towards the acidic. ◑, E, 10 × 15cm/4 × 6in

Corydalis flexuosa The popularity of this perennial remains undiminished. Above pretty, fern-like foliage appear clear blue flowers in the springtime. Position out of the full sun in a semi-shaded spot. 30 × 30cm/1 × 1ft

Brunnera macrophylla The Siberian bugloss makes excellent ground cover in the spring garden. Flowers, closely resembling a type of forget-me-not, are carried over strong, slightly felted foliage. Cut to the ground at the year's end. ◑, 45 × 60cm/1.5 × 2ft

Muscari aucheri As the flower spikes so clearly show, this form of the grape hyacinth is aptly named Oxford and Cambridge. Bulbs will steadily increase if left undisturbed to provide a mass of vivid colour each spring. 10–15cm/4–6in

Veronica pinnata **'Blue Eyes'** Plant this striking summer-flowering perennial at the front of a border or, as here, where it may fall over a low, retaining wall. Such a support prevents the plant from flopping outwards from the middle. ○, 20 × 30cm/8in × 1ft

Iris missouriensis Where soil is moisture retentive, then this lovely lavender-blue iris will thrive to delight with a fine show of blooms in the early summer. Sword-like leaves will remain as a foil to other plantings. 60 × 60cm/ 2 × 2ft

Veronica teucrium **'Shirley Blue'** Unfussy as to situation, thriving equally well in both sun and partial shade, this useful perennial flowers profusely throughout the summer. In this garden it forms an attractive edging to a stone path. 20 × 30cm/8in × 1ft

Iris sibirica **'Soft Blue'** Perennial irises like this one of pale blue are invaluable as border plants for the late spring into the first part of summer. In time clumps will increase, at which point they may be lifted and divided. 80 × 60cm/2.5 × 2ft

Rosmarinus officinalis Common rosemary need not be confined to the herb garden. This small shrub is deserving of a place in the mixed border, not just for its blue flowers but also for its very pleasing grey-green leaves. ○, E, 1.5 × 1.5m/5 × 5ft

Ceanothus impressus Grow this evergreen shrub for its deep blue flowers which cover a mature bush each springtime. Take care in winter for a heavy fall of snow will easily cause branches to split or break off completely. ○, E, 1.5 × 3m/5 × 10ft

***Ceanothus* 'Blue Mound'** In a small garden, where space is possibly at a premium, then this shrub is ideal. Of dwarf habit, forming an evergreen dome, the mid-blue flowers appear from the late spring into the early summer. Try training a later flowering clematis over the bush to extend the period of interest. All ceanothus benefit from shelter and good drainage and are generally unsuitable for gardens which are on shallow chalk. ○, E, 30 × 60cm/1 × 2ft

Camassia leichtlinii Violet-blue flowers arranged in spikes rise out of lush, clump-forming foliage in the early summer. This perennial appreciates moisture retentive soil which is not allowed to dry out. May be grown in grass in a wild garden. 75 × 30cm/2.5 × 1ft

Campanula latiloba Wonderful pyramidal spires of rich blue bring a vibrancy to summer borders. At this time of year true blue is hard to come by so perennial schemes based on this colour will, almost certainly, have to include those blues which are on the violet side of the colour wheel. 60 × 60cm/2 × 2ft

***Delphinium belladonna* 'Lamartine'** Perennial delphiniums are one of the mainstays of the garden in the months of summer. Tall, erect stems, which may well require some form of staking, give much needed height and stature to borders. A second crop of flowers is not unusual if spent spikes are cut off. This named variety is of a soft, mid-blue. Look out for the double, *Delphinium* 'Alice Artindale', which is an absolute joy but, sadly, not always readily available. 1.5m × 60cm/5 × 2ft

Felicia amelloides A tender perennial which is probably best treated as an annual. These clear blue flowers, with their cheery yellow centres, add sparkle to the border throughout the summer. Grow them also in pots and containers. ○, 45 × 45cm/1.5 × 1.5ft

Clematis durandii One of the easiest and most rewarding of clematis. These flowers of indigo-blue cover the plant from midsummer until well into autumn. Of fairly restricted growth, it may be trained over a small hoop as shown here. 1–1.2m/3–4ft

Anchusa azurea **'Loddon Royalist'** One of the truest of all blues for the first part of summer. Grow this perennial in full sun and associate with bearded irises and lupins for a dazzling effect. Some staking may be necessary. 1.2 × 60cm/4 × 2ft

Campanula latifolia Mauve-blue flowers mass this perennial in summer. A versatile bellflower for its ability to shine in a shady spot on heavy soil. But take care, flowers will seed around in a somewhat uncontrolled fashion. 1m × 60cm/3 × 2ft

Campanula cochleariifolia Fairy's thimble forms a low mat of dainty, nodding bells in midsummer. A tiny perennial suitable for the rock garden or to grow in gravel as pictured here. 10 × 60cm/4in × 2ft

Salvia patens Royal blue flowers are cooled by fresh green foliage on this summer-flowering perennial. Unfortunately, in all but the warmest of areas, this particular salvia is not hardy so cuttings must be taken to guarantee survival. 60 × 45cm/2 × 1.5ft

***Hydrangea macrophylla* 'Blue Wave'** Shades of the palest lilac-blue colour the florets of this late summer flowering shrub. As with all of the hydrangeas, the exact colour depends very much on the nature of the soil. The greater the acidity, the more intense the blue. Even when placed in full shade, you may still enjoy a mass of wonderful blooms. These may be brought indoors, dried and used as a focal point in winter arrangements. 2 × 2.7m/6 × 9ft

Huge flower heads of hydrangeas, although slightly uncompromising in shape, do, nonetheless, add a certain flamboyancy to end of summer season borders. Plant together to form a hedge or grow in containers which should be kept well watered.

***Ceanothus* 'Autumnal Blue'** A late summer and early autumn flowering shrub which, of all the ceanothus, may be counted amongst the hardiest. In format it is less dense than many of the others. ○, E, 4 × 4m/13 × 13ft

Platycodon grandiflorus mariesii Open panned flowers line the stems of this seldom seen perennial in summer. Closely akin to a campanula, the balloon flower will tolerate most situations apart from complete shade. As with so many herbaceous perennials, attention to dead heading will, in all likelihood, result in more flowers. Whatever, this task routinely carried out will help to maintain the appearance of the border. 60 × 45cm/2 × 1.5ft

Allium beesianum One of the onion family, this charmingly coloured bulbous plant flowers amongst thin, finely cut leaves. Plant to full gaps in between other summer-flowering perennials. 45cm/1.5ft

***Agapanthus* Headbourne Hybrids** From strap-like foliage emerge large flowerheads in summer. Bulbs of this agapanthus are exceedingly hardy and provide a wonderful show of colour. Grow either in the open ground or in pots. ○, 60 × 45cm/2 × 1.5ft

Ceratostigma plumbaginoides The hardy plumbago is one of the loveliest of shrubs for its exciting cobalt blue flowers which appear in the early autumn at a time when flames are in the ascendency. Position where it will catch the sun in dry, well drained soil. In cold areas stems are likely to be cut back to ground level. Well worth growing if at all possible. 1 × 1.5m/3 × 5ft

Perovskia atriplicifolia Russian sage is a shrub to enjoy in the later part of the summer when long panicles of pastel blue flowers are set off by grey-green foliage. Prune back hard in the early spring. 1 × 1.5m/3 × 5ft

Nicandra physalodes The shoo-fly plant, a hardy annual, carries attractive, bell-shaped flowers in late summer which are followed by ornamental Chinese lanterns of a papery quality. A handsome, vigorous plant. 1–1.2m/3–4ft

Caryopteris × *clandonensis* Often known as blue spiraea, this small shrub is valued for its late blue flowers over slightly glaucous leaves. Cut back each spring as flowers are carried on the current season's growth. ○, 80 × 80cm/ 2.5 × 2.5ft

Picea pungens '**Koster**' Evergreen conifers are much prized by many for the way in which they contribute form and interest in all seasons. The leaves of this pine are an intense silvery–blue, appearing most spectacular during winter months. E, 13 × 8m/43 × 26ft

CONSIDER ALSO:

SHRUBS:
Hibiscus syriacus 'Bluebird' (late summer)
Juniperus horizontalis 'Wiltonii' (evergreen)
Rosmarinus repens 'Severn Sea' (spring)

Linum perenne (summer)
Pulmonaria angustifolia 'Munstead Blue' (spring)
Salvia uliginosa (autumn)
Veronica peduncularis 'Georgia Blue' (spring/summer)

ANNUALS:
Consolida orientalis (Larkspur)
Ipomoea purpurea (Morning glory)
Nigella damascena (Love-in-a-mist)
Phacelia campanularia

BULBS:
Iris reticulata 'Harmony' (winter)
Muscari neglectum (spring)
Scilla sibirica 'Spring Beauty' (spring)

CLIMBERS:
Aconitum volubile (late summer)
Clematis 'Lasurstern' (spring/summer)

PERENNIALS:
Convolvulus sabatius (summer/autumn)

Ilex meservae The blue holly takes its name from its distinctly blue foliage making it an excellent subject for a scheme of that colour. All hollies are, of course, valuable for the textural quality they provide. E, 3 × 2.4m/10 × 8ft

Green

Of all the colours in the garden green is, for some extraordinary reason, the least valued. Indeed, in many instances it is, at best, regarded simply as a necessary background colour or, at worst, dismissed altogether. Featuring so often, and in so many guises, its true worth has almost completely become overlooked. Yet green is the most restful of colours which, acting as a foil to others, brings order, harmony and certain restraint to even the most restless of schemes.

That apart, it brings with it wonderful variation of form and texture to be found in both leaf and flower alike. For green encompasses so much. It is the colour of so many grasses, of ferns, of sedges and bamboos, of trees and shrubs unfurling new, precious shoots in the early spring as well as the bold sentinels of evergreens dominating the winter landscape. Green flowers give a subtlety to borders for they are understated and often,

delightfully, unexpected. And their range is by no means limited or restricted. There are eryngiums, euphorbias, galtonias, hellebores and tobacco plants (*Nicotiana*), as well as, surprisingly, primulas, red hot pokers and a rose.

Formal, structured gardens, where flowers may appear inappropriate, depend almost in their entirety on form provided by such plants as clipped box, yew, Portuguese laurel (*Prunus lusitanica*), hollies and ivies as well, of course, as grass with which to set off the whole effect.

It is not, of course, to everyone's taste to have a green garden. However, a more widespread acceptance of the value of green as a colour in its own right will, almost certainly, bring about a much needed reappraisal of the way in which, with imagination and thought, gardens may be developed if not transformed.

This corner of a terrace relies very heavily on green plants, both for their form and texture, to create an effect which is restful to the eye and yet is not without interest. Leathery leaves of bergenia contrast with the soft, floating flowers of the lady's mantle, *Alchemilla mollis*, which, in turn, is set against a stand of dark green foliage. The clipped box in the half barrel serves to unite the various plantings.

Garrya elliptica An evergreen shrub noted for its long panicles of catkins which appear over the winter months. These are most apparent on male plants. Garrya, which will suffer in severe winters, is best given the shelter of a wall. E, 4 × 3m/13 × 10ft

Helleborus argutifolius This perennial favourite is a delight in the early part of the year with its flowers of the palest of greens set above sharp-toothed leaves which remain attractive throughout each season. Protect from cold winds. E, 60 × 90cm/2 × 3ft

Euphorbia characias ssp. ***wulfenii*** **'Lambrook Gold'** Selected in the 1950s, this fine form of spurge has, understandably, retained its popularity as a garden plant. Tall yellow flowers appear like spires in spring over cool green foliage. 1.2m × 1m/4 × 3ft

Dark green yew, always a most satisfying background, sets off these late flowering, viridiflora tulips, *Tulipa* 'Spring Green'. Combined with these is the low growing *Euphorbia polychroma*, its acid yellow and green bracts nicely complementing the colour of the tulips. In this garden setting, the 'Spring Green' are massed in a narrow border which runs alongside a grass path. Keeping to a single variety avoids a confused, muddled appearance and is kinder on the eye.

An unusual, original and highly imaginative use of fennel. Here its soft, feathery foliage is contrasted with the spiky flower stems and coarse leaves of an eryngium. Note how the planting is on a generous scale designed to create impact.

Illustrated here is one of the ways in which leaves of different shapes and sizes may be grouped together to create harmonious pictures. This composition is principally made up of *Heuchera* 'Greenfinch', *Iris pseudacorus* and *Rheum alexandrae*.

Smyrnium perfoliatum Yellow-green flowers of this summer perennial give limitless scope to both gardeners and flower arrangers alike. An interesting feature is the way in which the stems appear to grow through the circular leaves. 1m × 60cm/3 × 2ft

Euphorbia × martinii A perennial spurge with finely divided flower spikes which appear from early summer onwards. Place in a sunny spot for best results. All stems of euphorbia contain a sap which can irritate the skin. 60 × 30cm/2 × 1ft

Bupleurum angulosum A most unusual and much admired perennial for its flowers of pale green silk over strap–like leaves. Place in sun at the front of the border to act as a foil to other plantings. 60 × 30cm/2 × 1ft

Seedheads of crown imperials extend the period of interest of these bulbous plants from spring into summer. The flowers, normally of orange or yellow, take on a new lease of life as the seed pods ripen.

These mixed conifers are highlighted in this garden by a broad sweep of lady's mantle which produces lime-green flowers throughout the summer months. Gathered, and taken indoors, it is a most effective perennial for use in flower arrangements. *Alchemilla mollis* has a habit of self-seeding rather too freely. It is wise to cut off spent flowers as they go over to avoid young seedlings taking over the border. 45 × 45cm/1.5 × 1.5ft

Stipa tenuissima This beautiful and graceful perennial grass looks particularly pleasing in late summer when its slight plumes of feathery flowers are produced. Most magical of all when caught in the evening sunlight. ◯, 60 × 45cm/ 2 × 1.5ft

Euphorbia sikkimensis A splendid foliage plant for the back of a mixed border where its lime-green bracts will shine for many weeks in summer. Emerging shoots each spring are brilliant red in colour. 1m × 75cm/3 × 2½ft

Nicotiana Green flowered tobacco plants make an eye-catching display for summer borders. This annual is not completely hardy so should not be planted out until after the last of the frosts in late spring. 1m × 30cm/3 × 1ft

Eucomis bicolor An exotic looking perennial for a warm, sunny position where it will produce huge strappy leaves and tall spires of pale green rosette bracts, each one flashed with maroon, in late summer. O, 45 × 60cm/1.5 × 2ft

Adiantum venustum Plant the deciduous maidenhair fern along the banks of a small stream to enjoy its delicate, lace-like foliage which may be relied upon to appear fresh and attractive at all times. 25 × 25cm/10 × 10in

Polystichum setiferum 'Divisilobum' Flat fronds of the shield fern can, on occasion, give the appearance of having been lightly edged in silver. Not only is it evergreen but it is also tolerant of dry conditions. E, 1.2m × 1m/4 × 3ft

Veratrum nigrum Leaves of this perennial are of particular interest. Appearing as cup-shaped goblets, they open out as broad, variegated surfaces through which rise the muted, late summer flowers. Amongst the most desirable of garden plants. 1.5m × 60cm/5 × 2ft

Laurus nobilis Bay lends itself to clipping into shapes or may simply be grown in a sheltered spot as a handsome, evergreen shrub. It is equally suitable for pot cultivation. Enjoys full sun. 7 × 2m/23 × 6ft

***Hebe cupressoides* 'Boughton Dome'** Like a miniature yew buttress, this fine, dark green hebe makes up for any lack of flowers by being evergreen and, in maturity, shapely. Placed within a mixed border it contributes year-round form. Here it is positioned in such a way as to tower above and over a carpet of flowering thymes. Try growing a number of plants together to form a piece of living garden sculpture. 75 × 75cm/2.5 × 2.5ft

Miscanthus 'Silver Feather' An excellent foil to many other plants. Glossy green leaves, with white variegation, are followed in late summer with bronze plumes, not dissimilar to those of the pampas grass. 2m × 60cm/6 × 2ft

Pseudosasa japonica Bamboo, such as this, make lovely specimen plants for the border where they add height and structure. Evergreen, with tapering leaves, it produces a thicket of canes in time. 5m/15ft indefinite spread

Phormium tenax One of the most striking of all garden plants for effect, the evergreen phormium, with its sword–like leaves, is a must for the gardener who enjoys the dramatic. Here a pair stand guard to a partially concealed entrance, their stature somehow enhanced further by the frosty, wintry conditions. During very cold winters it may prove wise to gather them together in the protection of some old sacking. 3 × 1m/10 × 3ft

***Hebe* × *divergens* 'Edinensis'** The architectural quality of this evergreen shrub should not be overlooked. Its rotund habit and compact size make it suitable for inclusion in the smallest of gardens or as a specimen on a scree bed surrounded by a selection of carefully chosen alpine plants. In this picture it has been caught heavily laden with frost, thus capturing one of the delights of winter. 30cm × 1m/ 1 × 3ft

Salvia officinalis Evergreen, shrubby sage is a must for all with its wonderfully aromatic leaves. This is a plant which should be positioned where it may readily be touched in a sunny spot. 1 × 1m/3 × 3ft

Tanacetum vulgare The finely cut, crisp leaves of this tansy make it highly decorative throughout the season. In late summer tall-growing flowers are produced, heightening its value. Ideal in the kitchen or herb garden. 1m × 60cm/ 3 × 2ft

Variegation

Variegation in plants, usually to be found in foliage, provides an element of variety within the garden and is popular with gardeners very often as a means of brightening some otherwise gloomy or dark corner. Brought about by a chlorophyll deficiency in the main, variegated plants have in recent times been avidly collected by enthusiasts eager to give to their gardens something a little bit different. If there is any danger in this, then it lies in over-planting where too many variegated plants, placed too closely together, can give an impression of confusion and a general busyness which is not altogether desirable. Much greater harmony overall will be found where plants with variegation are used sparingly, perhaps singly, or as part of a carefully thought out, colour-themed border.

Green, yellow, cream, silver and white are the colours which appear, in various mixes, most frequently in variegated foliage. All combinations are inclined from time to time to revert to plain green, most often those which carry the blotch of non-green at the centre of the leaf rather than around the edges. Where individual leaves, or even whole stems or branches, do revert, then these should be cut out immediately they are first spotted.

Weigela florida **'Variegata'** This lively shrub appears fresh throughout the summer months on account of its impressive, cool green and white foliage. Arching branches of peachy-pink flowers in early summer make it ideal for a variety of situations, both in the flower garden as well as in the shrubbery. Care should be exercised to place it to advantage. Possibly at its best when surrounded with other plantings of plain green. 1.5 × 1.5/5 × 5ft

Euonymus fortunei **'Silver Queen'** One of the many variegated euonymus. This one has crisp green and ice-white leaves which are evergreen. Plant for year-round interest and effect. E, 2.4 × 1.5m/8 × 5ft

Euonymus fortunei **'Emerald 'n' Gold'** Much of the continued popularity of this shrub has to be on account of its colourful, golden foliage which will lift a mixed border in all seasons. E, 1 × 1.5m/3 × 5ft

Cornus alba **'Elegantissima'** Sparkling leaves of this dogwood may be used to lighten a dull spot in the garden or be used as a basis for an all white scheme. Normally forming a rounded bush, it may with careful pruning be grown as a standard with a clipped mophead. To encourage its red stems, and where space is restricted, prune it hard to the ground in the early part of the spring. 3 × 4m/ 10 × 13ft

Ilex aquifolium **'Argentea Marginata Pendula'** All the hollies are useful for providing out-of-season colour. This one, with its strikingly variegated foliage, has the additional bonus of a good crop of berries. E, 2.4 × 2.4m/8 × 8ft

Leucothoe walteri **'Rainbow'** A low growing, variegated shrub which deserves to be more widely planted. Pink, cream and yellow tinted leaves are accompanied in early summer by tiny white flowers. 75cm × 1m/2.5 × 3ft

Aralia elata **'Variegata'** Silver-white leaves of the highly desirable Japanese angelica tree present a picture of space and light. A hardy tree, it merits a warm situation where the new foliage is unlikely to be caught by a late frost. In the late summer it is massed with white flowers. This is one of the aristocrats of all shrubs and is exceedingly worthy of cultivation. 3.5 × 3m/12 × 10ft

Aucuba japonica **'Gold Dust'** Of all shrubs the aucubas may be relied upon to thrive in difficult situations. Planted in shade, and even dry soil, they will still endeavour to give of their best. E, 2.4 × 2.4m/8 × 8ft

Lonicera japonica **'Aureoreticulata'** The chief attraction of this compact honeysuckle is its leaves which are closely netted with yellow. Grow it for foliage rather than flower for it is reluctant to bloom. 3m/10ft

Acer negundo **'Flamingo'** The appeal of this deciduous tree has to be the variegation of the leaves. Distinctly marked white, green and pink they create an eye-catching display from spring until autumn. Look out for any branches which show signs of reverting These should immediately be cut out. A contained tree, 'Flamingo' is suitable for the smaller garden and looks well in most situations. 8 × 6m/26 × 20ft

Hosta **'Frances Williams'** Like huge dinner plates, the leaves of this cultivated plantain lily make a bold statement in the garden. Lime-green is matched in equal parts with grey-green for an unusual combination. 75 × 75cm/ 2.5 × 2.5ft

Hedera colchica **'Sulphur Heart'** Bold splashes of gold colour the vibrant green of this evergreen, climbing ivy. Most useful when placed to bring a touch of brilliance to an otherwise dark or uninteresting corner. E, 4.5m/15ft

Brunnera macrophylla **'Dawson's White'** In maturity these spring-flowering perennials make an excellent plant for moist beds and borders. Furthermore, even in partial shade they will reward with attractive blue flowers. ○, 45 × 60cm/1.5 × 2ft

Hedera helix **'Goldheart'** This evergreen favourite ivy really is alight with colour throughout the year and can, in the right spot, resemble a series of candles illuminating a dark room. Cut out any leaves which revert. E, 9m/30ft

***Houttuynia cordata* 'Chameleon'** This showy, ground-cover perennial is all too often overlooked as an interesting plant for the garden. With such exciting foliage, flashed with red, yellow and green, it makes a lovely addition to the water garden where it enjoys moisture retentive soil. Having said that, it may also be grown in a container where its spreading habit is kept in check. ○, 10cm/4in, indefinite spread

***Thymus* 'Doone Valley'** Tiny aromatic flowers and leaves have made thyme an enduring plant for people's use. This one, with its almost lemon foliage, looks spectacular as a part of a thyme carpet. 10cm/4in

***Spartina pectinata* 'Aureomarginata'** The graceful prairie cord grass has long, ribbon-like leaves edged with yellow. For best results, plant close to water with room to spread as it can prove to be invasive. 1.8m/6ft

White, Grey and Black

Gardening in this range makes its own demands on the gardener's skill, but white flowers and grey leaves, for example, are vital components of the plantsman's palette, though black tends to be more of a sought-after oddity.

White

White, the symbol of purity, innocence and perfection continues, more than any other colour in the garden, to hold the position of utmost supremacy. White flowers in absolute plenty carry with them a richness married with, paradoxically, a quiet, gentle sophistication. It is hardly surprising, therefore, that there has been such a preponderance in recent times of white borders and whole gardens. Unfortunately, the perfection that these schemes aspire to is often, rather sadly, completely elusive. What is not generally realized or appreciated is that the handling of white in the garden is more complex, more demanding than is the case with any other colours.

To be totally successful, white, unless used as a highlight, requires its own space, possibly within some secret and enclosed area where its impact will be absolute and complete. For this a background of formally arranged, clipped yew is ideal. Where this is not a possibility, then a boundary clothed in some dark evergreen, such as ivy, would suffice as well. Within this enclosure light plays an important role. Overhead daylight with the presence of a strong summer sun will do little for the colours beyond reducing them to a uniform drabness. To excel, they must enjoy the benefit of shade, becoming most pronounced, and at their loveliest, as the twilight of evening gathers. It is then too that any scent, for many white flowers are particularly perfumed, will be most fragrant and most noticeable.

Probably one of the most famous of all white gardens, this one at Sissinghurst Castle in Kent was created by Vita Sackville-West in the years immediately following the Second World War. In its time it has become an inspiration for others and remains highly regarded.

Serving as a focal point is the silver-leafed pear, *Pyrus salicifolia* 'Pendula', which picks up the tones of the silvery perennials to be found in the surrounding borders.

Helleborus niger The Christmas rose brings cheer to the garden in the early part of the year. A worthwhile perennial for its foliage remains looking good for the entire season. Plant in rich soil in a slightly shaded situation. E, ○, 45 × 45cm/1.5 × 1.5ft

Narcissus **'Flower Drift'** Papery white petals set off a centre of rich egg-yolk yellow in this spring-flowering bulb. Many of the white flowered daffodils would be most suitable for a pale scheme. 45 × 45cm/1.5 × 1.5ft

Camellia japonica **'Nobilissima'** The pure white flowerhead of this early camellia is particularly enticing. All of these shrubs are best positioned away from the early morning sun which can cause browning after a night of frost. E, 3 × 2m/10 × 6ft

Syringa vulgaris A white form of the common lilac for spring colour. Sweetly scented blooms are especially good gathered for an indoor arrangement. Where possible, dead-head before flowers die off. A hardy shrub. 6 × 4m/ 20 × 13ft

Erythronium californicum **'White Beauty'** Erythroniums are especially attractive spring bulbs for a lightly shaded area in humus-rich soil. This white flowered one has strikingly marked foliage. Plant in the autumn for spring flowering. ◐, 30 × 20cm/1ft × 8in

Tulipa **'Purissima'** Spring-flowering bulbs are a must in any garden. These creamy-white tulips look particularly effective planted among daffodils, primula and variegated honesty, *Lunaria annua alba*, in this cool border scheme. 40 × 20cm/16 × 8in

Anemone blanda **'White Splendour'** Scatter these tiny bulbs beneath shrubs and trees to enjoy the delicate flowers in the spring. Left undisturbed they will naturalize over a period of time to form a white carpet. 10cm/4in

Prunus **'Tai Haku'** The Great White Cherry is spectacular in flower and is well worth including in the garden even though the blossom is soon over. The tree itself matures into an attractive, spreading shape. 8 × 8m/26 × 26ft

Viburnum plicatum **'Mariesii'** Flat white flower corymbs distinguish this attractive and easily grown shrub in the late spring and first part of the summer. May be grown as a specimen or included as part of a mixed border. 3 × 4m/10 × 13ft

Geranium macrorrhizum **'Album'** A spreading, hardy perennial to use as ground cover under and around trees and shrubs. This white form of cranesbill would look particularly pleasing placed within an informal setting or drifting through an all white border in early summer. 60 × 60cm/2 × 2ft

Tiarella cordifolia Plant this woodland perennial in soil which will not dry out. Feathery white racemes appear from the late spring well into early summer, after which leaves remain fresh and green. 30 × 30cm/1 × 1ft

Libertia formosa Above tall, strap-like leaves rise tiny flowers of the purest of whites throughout the spring. A totally hardy perennial which is best cut back hard to the ground during the late winter. Semi-E, 1 × 1m/3 × 3ft

Wisteria floribunda **'Alba'** Amongst the aristocrats of climbers, wisteria is grown not only for its beautiful long flower racemes which appear in early summer but also for its interesting, twisted stems. ○, 9m/30ft

Cistus **'Paladin'** A shrub for a hot, dry, sunny site. Paper-white flower petals surrounding deep yellow stamens are blotched a deep wine red and are carried over glossy, dark green leaves. The additional colouring excites interest. ○, E, 2 × 2m/6 × 6ft

Most of the cistus are suitable for growing on chalk. Among named forms is the white flowered *Cistus × hybridus* also in bloom from early to midsummer.

Centranthus ruber albus That the white perennial valerian is likely to seed around at will is no real disadvantage in any but the smallest of gardens. It will be a source of continuous colour from early summer onwards. 1m × 45cm/3 × 1.5ft

Sidalcea candida A flowering period stretching from early summer through until the start of autumn makes this herbaceous perennial a welcome addition to the garden. Unfussy about situation it can look wonderful when paired with *Melianthus major*. 1m × 75cm/3 × 2.5ft

A lovely, informal grouping of white flowered perennials alongside a path made up of random flints. Note how young seedlings are permitted to come through the cracks, adding to the already relaxed atmosphere. Included here are *Lychnis coronaria* 'Alba', a pale astrantia and white poppies.

Although planting of this kind appears easy to achieve there is, in fact, a great deal of skill required in maintaining a balance between deliberately planned informality and chaos.

Iris orientalis A most striking perennial iris with white falls coloured deep yellow. Equally attractive in bud when green-tinged stripes are noticeable. To be found flowering in the late spring and early summer. 60 × 60cm/2 × 2ft

Nicotiana Often selected for summer bedding, the fragrant tobacco plant is most usually grown as an annual although self-set seedlings will sometimes come through a mild winter. Plant in sun. Pictured here is a desirable white variety. 30 × 15cm/1ft × 6in

***Rosa* 'Iceberg'** Early summer is the time for roses. Of all the floribunda shrub roses it is hardly surprising that 'Iceberg' retains its popularity. These icy blooms, which appear for an extended season, are marvellous for sustaining colour in an all white garden. 1.2 × 1.2m/ 4 × 4ft

In order to avoid leggy growth, it is best to prune this rose hard, rather in the manner of a hybrid tea, over the winter at which time a mulch of well rotted compost may be applied.

Lilium regale Summer-flowering lilies, deeply scented, are one of the joys of the garden. This one, amongst the finest, is certainly no exception. Seen here, it is planted into a border where, given good drainage, the bulbs will continue to flower for many years. 1.2m/4ft

Lilies do, of course, make excellent subjects for containers and pots. They may be brought into prominence during the flowering period and then removed out of the way once it is over.

Lilium 'Olivia' Placed against a background of dark yew, this white lily positively shines. What is also demonstrated here is the way in which all bulbous lilies may be successfully grown in pots. This one is particularly fine and made of terracotta. 1.2m/4ft

Campanula latiloba alba White bells cluster around stiffly held stems over evergreen, basal rosettes. Summer-flowering, this is a perennial for any white garden or border or to be used to cool down somewhat sharper tones. Remove spent flower spikes to maintain a tidy appearance. 1.2m × 30cm/4 × 1ft

Campanula persicifolia The white form of this trouble-free perennial, in flower in midsummer, is emphasized by the blue with which it is teamed in this border. Sometimes, even when using a single colour, it makes sense to introduce another sparingly. ○, 1m × 30cm/3 × 1ft

***Clematis viticella* 'Little Nell'** When considering climbers clematis do, very naturally, come to mind. This late summer viticella is essentially white with pale pink bands at the outer edges of the petals. Hard prune over winter. 3–3.6m/10–12ft

Leucanthemum* × *superbum Shasta daisies are tough, versatile herbaceous perennials with which to fill late summer borders. Divide clumps periodically when they become woody and overcrowded. Most will continue to flower well into the autumn. 1.2 × 1m/4 × 3ft

Malva moschata alba An easy little perennial which will spread outwards in most normal garden soils. Useful for placing close to trees and shrubs as an easily controlled form of summer-flowering ground cover. 60 × 60cm/ 2 × 2ft

An ethereal, even haunting quality, is achieved here in this white section of a large herbaceous border. Tall, almost see-through spires of *Veronicastrum virginicum* provide a backdrop to the stiff, rather paper-like flowers of the lower growing *Anaphalis margaritacea*. Both plants share similar grey-green foliage.

Perennials, planted closely together as these have been, virtually eliminate the need for any weeding during the growing season. They also look much more effective.

Anemone* × *hybrida Japanese anemones must be amongst the most accommodating of all garden plants. Perennial and hardy, they cover the ground for the greater part of the year with not unattractive leaves and then flower for weeks on end from late summer onwards. 1.5m × 60cm/ 5 × 2ft

Towards the end of the winter cut dead stems and spent foliage to ground level. Within a short space of time new growth will emerge.

***Echinacea purpurea* 'White Swan'** One of the most admired of all late summer perennials most likely on account of its green tinted petals and centre of similar colour. Cone flowers will thrive in most garden soils and will tolerate a degree of light shade. 1.2m × 75cm/ 4 × 2.5ft

It is worth taking the time and trouble to deadhead perennials on a regular basis. They will certainly repay this work with a prolonged flowering period.

***Artemisia lactiflora* Guizhou Group** Strong, near black stems support light, airy flowers on this herbaceous perennial which, rather surprisingly, is as well suited to the front of the border as it is to the rear. Serrated leaves add to its attraction. 1m × 60cm/3 × 2ft

Cosmos Include annual white cosmos in summer bedding schemes or to be grown as a cutting flower for the house. This variety appears to capture total innocence. In common with most annuals grown for summer colour, cosmos prefers a sunny spot. 60cm/2ft

***Crinum* × *powellii* 'Album'** Bulbs of late summer crinums prefer to be planted in a sheltered position, possibly against a wall, in full sun and to be given free draining soil. That said, they are not difficult to cultivate. ○, 1m × 60cm/ 3 × 2ft

Crinums are not at all difficult to raise from seed. Large seeds should be sown three or four to a pot following a period in cold storage.

Magnolia grandiflora Most often the magnolias are thought of as spring-flowering. This slow growing variety, which will eventually become a large tree, blooms at the end of summer. This is a handsome plant deserving of a choice position. E, 10 × 10m/33 × 33ft

Dahlia Dahlias are once more back in fashion even though, on account of their not being frost hardy, they require a little effort to be taken over their cultivation. This spidery white one with lemon centre is particularly fine. Most flower at the year's end From 30cm/1ft

Gladiolus These showy flowers for summer come from corms which are not in themselves hardy and so must be lifted when the first frosts occur. Rather uncompromising in the mixed border they are ideal to grow for flower arranging. ◯, 1.2m × 30cm/4 × 1ft

Cimicifuga simplex A late flowering perennial producing elongated spikes well into autumn. This is a plant to provide a variation of form within the border. Massed, it is almost certainly bound to elicit comment and to be noticed. 1m × 60cm/3 × 2ft

***Colchicum autumnale* 'Album'** These are tiny autumn-flowering bulbs, as their name would suggest, to naturalize in grass where they should increase as the years pass. This white variety is especially pleasing. 20 × 20cm/8 × 8in

---

CONSIDER ALSO:

SHRUBS:
Camellia 'Cornish Snow' (spring)
Carpenteria californica (summer)
Hibiscus syriacus 'Diana' (late summer/autumn)
Magnolia stellata 'Royal Star' (spring)
Romneya coulteri (summer–autumn)
Rosa rugosa alba (summer)

ANNUALS:
Argemone grandiflora
Lavatera trimestris 'Mont Blanc'

PERENNIALS:
Astilbe 'Deutschland' (summer)

Phlox paniculata 'White Admiral' (summer)
Pulmonaria officinalis 'Sissinghurst White' (spring)

BULBS:
Crocus chrysanthus 'Snow Bunting' (early spring)
Narcissus 'Thalia' (spring)
Tulipa 'White Triumphator' (spring)

CLIMBERS:
Clematis montana 'Grandiflora' (early summer)
Lathyrus latifolius 'White Pearl' (summer)
Rosa 'Climbing Iceberg' (summer)

Cyclamen hederifolium* f. *album Positively lovely to mass underneath a deciduous tree or shrub. These little bulbs, if left to their own devices, will steadily multiply in time to give much pleasure at the close of the year. 10 × 20cm/ 4 × 8in

Leaves are attractive in their own right. Following immediately after the flowers, they are ivy-shaped of silvery green.

Cortaderia selloana The magnificent plumes of the architectural pampas grass bring to the end of the year a certain grace and style. Belonging more to the large garden than the smaller one, they look lovely in association with water. 2 × 1.2m/6 × 4ft

Tough measures are called for if the pampas grass is to remain healthy and look good. Cut back hard to the ground each spring but wear strong gloves for this task as the leaves are razor sharp.

Grey

Grey, as a colour, may not at first appear particularly exciting. Yet within a garden setting it comes into its own and, far from seeming of little interest, time and again proves itself as being amongst the most versatile of colours. First and foremost, grey is invaluable for separating colours which do not combine well together and which, if juxtaposed, would result in the most horrible of clashes. In such a situation, which all too easily may arise at certain points in the garden as a whole if not within a single border, grey provides an interval and acts as a neutral agent.

Second, rather in the manner of white, grey helps to shape a border, to give it visual balance and form. A pool of grey, sited among other darker colours, will draw the eye and in so doing, albeit unconsciously, suggest definition and even purpose.

But, more than anything else, grey is such a wonderful partner to other plants. For a really moody, even gothic, effect, then combine it with deep purple or darkest magenta. Where a soft, dreamy picture is appropriate, then place it among pinks, lemons, lavenders and greens. For something much more startling and daring, mix grey with the lacquer red of a Chinese bridge or position it with the brown of a Russian bear. And, most difficult of all, use grey with black. The results are stunning!

Here grey is seen at its most architectural. The onopordum is deliberately chosen to tower over the alliums to give a sense of drama to this border which has been formally edged with box. Coolness of colour is especially welcome in the summer months when this scheme becomes a retreat from the hot shades of so many herbaceous perennials. Worth noting is the contrast made between the coarse-cut leaves of the onopordum and the leaf shape of the box.

Ghost-grey leaves of the curry plant, *Helichrysum italicum*, appear to float over the muted grey-green rue, *Ruta graveolens*, in this corner of a border. As the dianthus in the foreground spreads, so the overall effect will be complete.

Stachys byzantina, affectionately named lambs' ears, has been imaginatively used here in association with other grey leafed plants to highlight the purple foliage of *Lysimachia ciliata* 'Firecracker'. Grey grasses could also be included for further contrast of leaf.

Grey shrubs and perennials, used as these, help to create depth and space in a border. Placed with care they may also either highlight other plantings or, indeed, tone down those which may, in certain circumstances, approach the garish. Here height plays an important part in leading the eye onwards down the length of the border. By restricting the amount of other colour used in the same area, confusion is avoided.

Blue and grey successfully combine together, as illustrated here, to make for a cool interlude within a planting scheme. Not only do the mid-blues look well with grey, but also those which are darker. Pale shades need to be selected with care for fear of appearing washed out. For contrast of foliage, arrange the sword-like leaves of *Iris sibirica* 'Summer Sky' with feathery *Artemisia* 'Powis Castle'. More daring is *Cynara cardunculus* with *Stipa barbata* 'Silver Feather'.

Verbascum olympicum Mulleins are surely amongst the loveliest of perennials. Pale grey foliage of the young leaves surround tall flower spikes which, when fully open, appear to light a border like a series of giant candles.
2m × 60cm/6 × 2ft

Considering both form and texture in the garden is never easy and requires a certain amount of flair. In this instance Scotch thistles have been positioned with the spike-forming fox-tail lily, *Eremurus stenophyllus* ssp. *stenophyllus*.

Inspired planting is to be found in this grouping. Not only are the colours suggestive, but attention has been given to the detail of contrasting leaf shape and texture. Through the deep, plum-coloured leaves of the *Heuchera micrantha* 'Palace Purple' the finely cut foliage of the silvery *Artemisia* 'Powis Castle' appears to weave a magical spell. Like so many ideas, the simplest are often the best.

This anaphalis, shown in the foreground, brings a certain unity to the other colours in the border, ably assisted by the white flowered achillea. Tall growing shrubs in the background fulfil their purpose.

Generous plantings of fine grey foliage, such as is to be found on this tanacetum, are at their best when seen in contrast. Here this is made with a sedum whose leaves are an enviable claret colour.

A bold colour statement which cannot be denied. At the base of the burgundy cotinus a broad band of silver-leafed artemisia strikes a forceful contrast. To this is added gold in the form of the golden hop, *Humulus lupulus* 'Aureus', which may be relied upon to brighten up the dullest of days. The cotinus may be hard pruned each spring in order to promote new, richly coloured growth.

Scale in the garden is important. In this one a low wall is fronted with a series of the compact shrub, *Berberis thunbergii* 'Bagatelle', meeting to form a small hedge, which, in turn, is shown off by an extensive sweep of the non-flowering, *Stachys byzantina* 'Silver Carpet'. This kind of planting is simple, direct and effective and is not at all difficult to reproduce if not exactly the same, then similar.

Tall growing stachys, spilling out onto the grass, behind which is a grey artemisia, have been employed in this border to create a moment of respite amongst other varied colours. In this way the eye is given rest before advancing onwards.

Carpet bedding of this kind can, unless great care is taken, appear somewhat overwhelming. To counter this, cineraria, with its non-assertive grey leaves, has been included, rather in the way of a mark of punctuation within a sentence.

This cool, yet dramatic effect, has been made possible by the use of limited colours to produce an even display. Grey artemisia, *Artemisia ludoviciana* 'Valerie Finnis' mingles with the white flowers of an achillea and the butterfly blooms of *Gaura lindheimeri*, seen on the right. A note of acid green is introduced in the foliage of the very different, *Achillea grandifolia*. Although giving the impression of a random arrangement, this planting is, in fact, carefully staged.

Eryngium* × *zabelii Crowding the front of the border are these splendid, summer-flowering perennial plants with their steely, spiny flower heads, ideal for the flower arranger either fresh or dried. Such skeletal plants make for wonderful contrasts when placed with other fuller perennials such as *Zantedeschia aethiopica* 'Crowborough' or *Astilbe* 'Deutschland'. ◯, 45 × 25cm/1.5ft × 10in

Silver-grey artemisia acts as a screen in this corner of a border, turning an otherwise normally yellow anthemis into a beautiful antique gold. Taller growing plants do not always have to be dispatched to the back.

Tanacetum haradjanii This interesting tansy is grown for its most striking foliage. Contrast it with any dark flower to create an incident of pure theatre. ◯, 60 × 60cm/2 × 2ft

156

Here anaphalis has been extensively used as a backdrop to the soft pink and white, summer-flowering border phlox. All greys do, of course, associate well with pinks darkening to mauve and may be used successfully as underplanting and ground cover. Where space allows, consider the grey grass, *Elymus magellanicus*, which grows to around 1m/3ft. But be careful as it can be invasive.

Brachyglottis (Senecio) 'Sunshine' This evergreen shrub will, in time, form a compact dome. In summer it is covered in a mass of rather bright, yellow flowers which may, if you prefer, be cut off. ○, E, 1 × 1.5m/3 × 5ft

CONSIDER ALSO:

SHRUBS AND TREES:	
Ballota	*Eucalyptus gunnii*
Elaeagnus × *ebbingei*	*Juniperus horizontalis*
'Limelight'	'Wiltonii'
	Pyrus salicifolia 'Pendula'

Black

Black as a colour within the garden must, inevitably, be limited to flowers of the deepest, darkest hue, to foliage of a similar nature and to the stems and branches of many shrubs and trees, these last most apparent in wintertime. True, there are flowers which are named black, such as *Tulipa* 'Black Parrot', *Viola* 'Roscastle Black', *Scabiosa* 'Chile Black' and *Iris* 'Black Swan', but these are, in the main, in the minority. A really black grass, however, does exist, *Ophiopogon planiscapus* 'Nigrescens', sometimes known as Black Dragon, which is most effective when planted in a mass. But in most instances black is a constituent part of some other coloured plant, as in the eye of the *Rudbeckia*, commonly named Black-eyed Susan, or in the dark stems to be found in *Pittosporum × tenuifolium*.

The impact of black in the garden must lie in the way in which it is combined with other plants to create a sense of mystery, to give a feeling of style or to be used simply for sheer dramatic effect.

Tulipa **'Queen of the Night'** Tightly cupped tulips such as these near-black ones look especially striking placed against the silver-grey leaves of the cardoon, *Cynara cardunculus*. Once the flowers are over, deadhead and allow foliage to die down naturally. 45cm/1.5ft

Tulipa **'Black Parrot'** Almost impossible to go wrong with tulips the colour of these. Curly but crisp blooms in shades of dark purple-black are wonderfully atmospheric and capable of bringing a moment of drama to any border.

Plant in large groups for best results as tulips, and these are no exception, are so much better in a mass. Try them too in pots and containers to be taken indoors at flowering time. 45cm/1.5ft

Aquilegia vulgaris **'Magpie'** Columbines remain a perennial favourite. These, with flowers of muddied white and ink black, add a touch of difference to the front of the early summer border. Plant them with dark purples and mauves for a scheme which is a little out of the ordinary. 1m × 45cm/3 × 1.5ft

Viola **'Bowles' Black'** These charming little violets with their unusual black flowers are excellent to drift through borders. Grown at the base of a yew hedge they will reinforce a sombre, moody look. 10 × 30cm/4in × 1ft

Helleborus orientalis Hellebores with their evergreen foliage, are wonderful perennial plants for the spring. Seen in many different colours, dark shades, particularly near-black, are especially sought after and are, understandably, expensive to buy. ◑, E, 45 × 45cm/1.5 × 1.5ft

Ophiopogon planiscapus **'Nigrescens'** This perennial grass with black, sword-like leaves is so versatile for its ability to look effective with so many other plants. The flowers, tiny purple bells hidden among the foliage, are an added delight. 25 × 25cm/10 × 10in

159

Colour Combinations

The colour of one flower affects our perception of the colour of the flower next to it. En masse, colours can produce striking effects. Some of the most successful colour combinations are shown on the following pages.

Yellow with White

Soft, pale yellows, some of cool lemon and others of deep butter, are the colours of springtime and early summer. With them comes a satisfying warmth and a glowing brilliance, helping to establish a pattern for the rest of the year. Not for now the strong golds and ripened corn colours of late summer and autumn, but gentle, alluring tints which suggest rather than state. Teamed with white they take on a lightness of tone, creating an almost elusive radiance, becoming both precious and rather special.

Such a combination is seldom commonplace. It remains both subtle and suggestive, an understatement, demanding of close observation. Light in tone, somewhat ethereal even, these colours together are enticing to the eye and bring to the garden, simultaneously, both serenity and excitement. Enjoy them particularly in the evening as the light fades when they will take on a luminosity which is, at times, unforgettable.

Set against foliage of deeply-dark green, upright spires of verbascum positively glow in this summer scheme. Intermingling are drifts of feverfew, *Tanacetum parthenium*, the yellow eye of which exactly matches the flower of its taller companion. Clear white petals lift the entire scheme.

Rosa 'Canary Bird' and *Veronica gentianoides* 'Tissington White' are the principal players in this yellow and white spring border. Creamy *Aquilegia* 'Edelweiss' provides a link between the two. Reinforcing the white is *Centaurea montana alba* and an unusual variegated, perennial honesty. A rogue blue cornflower has crept into the plantings. In some respects this acts as a foil as well as heightening awareness of the dominant theme.

Wonderfully warm, butter-yellow heads of *Tulipa* 'Maréchal Niel' crown a carpet of white Universal pansies in this highly imaginative and very successful scheme. A gardener's eye for detail is apparent in the way in which the tiny speck of yellow at the centre of each pansy picks up the tulip colour. The pansies will, of course, have been in flower on and off throughout the entire winter.

Simple but effective. Open white blooms of *Rosa rugosa* 'Alba' are surrounded with a planting of the modest yellow and white feverfew (*Tanacetum parthenium*), with its acid-yellow, aromatic leaves.

Graceful white foxgloves soar over yellow whorls of the Jerusalem sage (*Phlomis fruticosa*), the whole scheme punctuated with the creamy yellow blooms of an early summer rose. A mellow brick wall provides a sympathetic background.

Colour has been carefully managed in this corner of a garden. Yellow, white, and of course green, have been gathered together to create an informal planting area which is not without interest but which remains restful to the eye and is undemanding of attention. Mats of creeping thyme enjoy a cool root run underneath the stones of the path and are in sharp contrast to the lady's mantle which edges the border.

Imagine this wonderfully warm coloured lily, *Lilium* 'Golden Splendor', adding a touch of the exotic to a white and yellow border. Lilies, like this one, which may be grown in open ground, prefer full sun and free draining soil. Because of this they are often best grown in pots which may, at flowering time, be sited in the border, later to be removed.

In this totally relaxed planting white honesty, *Lunaria annua alba*, a biennial, sparkles with creamy tulips in this display for the middle of spring.

White lilies with soft yellow centres stand out against the ice-blue eryngiums in this border comprised mainly of yellow with white. The addition of a hint of blue serves to highlight the overall scheme.

Yellow with Red

Employ these strong colours together to create schemes, if not whole borders, which are hot, fiery and challenging as well as being visually exciting. These are not shades to mix for those who like their gardens to be restful and easy on the eye, for they are certainly neither of these. However, where there is a will for change, a desire for something very different, then these are the colours to startle and surprise.

Setting is always important and never more so than when using primary colours together en masse. A plain, dark background will set off these colours and avoid the confusion likely to arise where they merge into or mingle with paler shades.

This is certainly a combination which is easy to achieve, and can be quite successful, later in the year when the strong reds and yellows of heleniums mix with the yellows of rudbeckias and reds of echinaceas.

Lime-yellow bracts of the *Euphorbia polychroma* give to the dusky-red flowers of *Geum rivale* a new and fresh look. Both may be planted at the front of the border as a novel approach to the early summer.

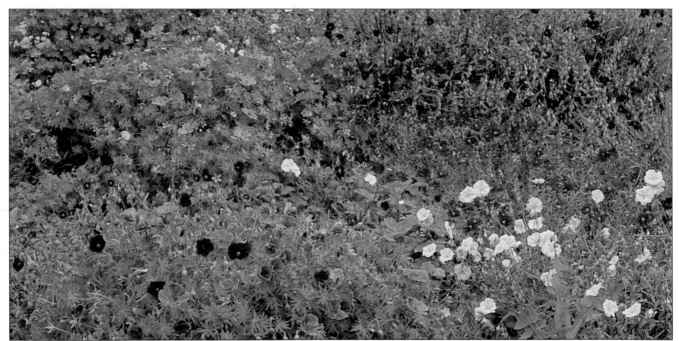

Orange, red and yellow helianthemums (rock roses) jostle together in this planting of early summer where the intention is to create a tapestry of colour. The pinky-mauve cranesbills, drawing on pastel shades, lead the eye away from the hot tones on the right side of the bed. Combining colours like this requires good knowledge of plants and careful planning.

Mahogany-red *Helenium* 'Moerheim Beauty' is toned down in this planting by combining it with creamy-yellow *Aconitum lycoctonum* ssp. *vulparia*. A very different effect would result if a stronger yellow had been used.

Wonderful claret-red lobelia, *Lobelia* 'Compliment Scarlet', tower over pale cream button heads of *Santolina chamaecyparissus* 'Lemon Queen' to bring about a contrast of colour as well as of shape and form.

With its soft, velvety foliage and creamy flowers *Verbascum nigrum* is the ideal companion to this blood-red, late summer helenium for end of season excitement. Not only are the flowers good in the garden but both would look most decorative arranged in a vase indoors where they would give pleasure for a considerable time. Verbascums may, of course, be successfully dried as they will retain their original colour.

Yellow with Blue and Purple

Yellow with blue is, of course, a classic combination. Put with purple it is possibly a little more unusual, but equally effective. The first is very much suggestive of the early part of the year, when drifts of daffodils may run through plantings of blue *Muscari* (grape hyacinth) or *Chionodoxa* (glory of the snow). The second comes into its own as summer gathers pace and a large range of yellow and purple subjects are available to the gardener. Yellow, in all its shades, is a colour which cannot be ignored, one to which the eye is automatically drawn. For this reason it needs to be sited with care. Linking it with another colour, such as blue, reduces its force and, if lemon is used, brings it into the pastel range. With purple, gold and deep tones, particularly, give a much stronger impression, a heaviness even, which may require a lift with white, grey or silver.

A charming drift of Welsh poppies, *Meconopsis cambrica*, together with flurries of forget-me-nots are the basis for this natural looking, spring planting scheme which conspires to produce one of the best colour combinations, that of yellow and blue.

Both these blue irises and yellow mimulus enjoy the moisture retentive soil to be found on this bankside. The white painted bench demonstrates very clearly how the eye is drawn to light colours in the garden.

Yellow hemerocallis (day lilies) planted in a drift have been artfully interspersed with pale china-blue cranesbill, the whole effect being set off by a thick wall of green foliage which will come into its own at a later stage.

Buttermilk anthemis, with broad, flat flowerheads, are well complemented in this arrangement by blue scabious. To this is added the thin, tube-like flowers of phygelius, a shrubby perennial which is best cut to the ground each spring.

Pale mauve *Campanula lactiflora* is teamed in this instance with the homely yellow of *Verbascum nigrum*. Of interest is the way in which the very centre of the campanula picks up the colour of the verbascum.

Delphiniums, those stalwarts of summer borders, are grown here with the pompon flowers of *Gentiana lutea*. To these could be added border phlox, in appropriate shades, to extend the season of interest.

Waving scabious flowers contrast here with the flat heads of achillea to produce a pleasing interlude within a mixed border. Behind, the stand of purple salvia adds a further dimension.

An attractive woodland scene in spring where the Welsh poppy, *Meconopsis cambrica*, intermingles freely with bluebells, *Hyacinthoides non-scriptus*, to form a carpet of colour. Both these perennials will self-seed so should be given space.

In this spring border, mainly consisting of blue and yellow, it is the yellows which are allowed to dominate and which, in the early part of the year, appear most vibrant. The brightest yellow are the leaves of *Valeriana phu* 'Aurea' at the front of the border.

Borders like this one, pictured in spring, have been planned with confidence. Colour is tightly controlled, in this case restricted to blue and yellow, and plants are packed closely together for the greatest possible impact. The large flowering shrub is *Kerria*. Interestingly, the whole scheme succeeds without the introduction of daffodils which here would be untidy in appearance once the flowers were over.

Midsummer, and this border of perennials is fully grown up. In this garden clear blue has been replaced with violet-blue, verging towards purple, accompanied by a citrus yellow. Flowers in the foreground are those of *Asphodeline lutea*.

The effect of massed planting is clearly demonstrated here in this splendid stand of *Coreopsis verticillata* against which is grown the steely-blue, thistle heads of *Eryngium × zabelii*. Both plants are perennial and fully hardy.

A summer border entirely given over to perennials in shades of blue, violet, yellow and cream. Bold clumps of *Anthemis tinctoria* 'E.C. Buxton' are placed at regular intervals with the express purpose of leading the eye onwards, whilst nepetas, salvias, echinops and helianthus, yet to flower, are included not simply for flower colour but also for variation of texture and form. All of these plants will be cut back to ground level during the late autumn.

Blue with White

Together these two colours make for wonderfully cool, even icy, schemes. This is a combination to follow an area of the garden which is devoted to warm shades or to terminate mixed plantings. Most often the same flower is to be found in both blue and white, and most effective schemes may be devised by using drifts of each in the same border. Among the most common are to be found agapanthus, campanulas, delphiniums, gentians and geraniums.

However, some caution should be exercised in the positioning of blue and white. Blue, unlike white, recedes and it is all too easy, especially when using paler shades, to finish up with an arrangement which is, in part, lacking in definition.

Rounded heads of border phlox are sharpened by the intense blue of the hardy agapanthus which is planted to grow up through them. Similarly shaped, they nevertheless work together to make an eye-catching display.

These white love-in-a-mist (*Nigella*) surround the palest of blue flowers of the *Polemonium* (Jacob's ladder), giving it an ethereal, romantic quality. In this way attention is drawn to the Jacob's ladder which might otherwise be overlooked.

A fine example to show the effect of mixing together the same plant but in different colours. Here the china blue and crystal white of *Campanula latifolia* have been massed in a border for a visually attractive display.

White may, on occasion, when put against other colours, appear rather too startling and out of place. Illustrated here is how, when used in a simple planting, it can enhance. Sweetly scented flowers of the Mexican orange blossom, *Choisya* 'Aztec Pearl', produce a swirling cloud through which rise tall spires of blue camassia, *Camassia leichtlinii*, so that they become an integral part of the shrub. Altogether, a choice and imaginative planting.

A most arresting scheme in which the cool white flowers of *Clematis montana* are juxtaposed with those of the mauve-blue *Abutilon × suntense*. Both will bloom in the late spring and early summer.

Growing to little more than 10 × 7.5cm/4 × 3in, *Anemone appenina* may be left undisturbed to naturalize a partly shaded area of the garden where it will produce myriads of starry flowers in springtime.

For a striking contrast in the late spring. *Clematis montana* has been trained through and among the powder-blue flowers of *Ceanothus* 'Blue Mound'. It should be remembered that this clematis type is exceedingly vigorous and care will need to be taken to see that it is not allowed to choke the host shrub. This particular ceanothus may not be fully hardy in a very cold area. An alternative would be *Ceanothus × thyrsiflorus*.

Although not strictly blue, the flowers of the charming yet unassuming violet, *Viola cornuta*, make a lovely contrast with the taller growing, white flowers of *Malva moschata alba*. Allowing violas to seed randomly through a border is one way of achieving a relaxed, almost careless effect which can be particularly effective in an informal situation. Weed out any which are misplaced.

Ice-white bells of *Campanula persicifolia* are placed here with the clear yellow flowers of a perennial potentilla. The long stems of the potentilla reach upwards into the campanula to make an informal arrangement.

Metallic eryngiums are partnered in this cool border with white eschscholtzia, an annual which will flower all through the symmer and well into autumn. Also included is the perennial *Sisyrinchium striatum* 'Aunt May' with its distinctive, variegated leaves.

Lavender with Pinks and Reds

Misty lavender-blues combine with quiet pinks and rich reds to produce borders of contemplative, pensive beauty through long summer months. These moody tints induce feelings of relaxation, of restfulness, of introspection even. They are a foil to harsh sunlight and the season's glare. With them comes a sense of peace, of tranquillity and harmony.

Such blues are non-assertive, lacking the intensity of a clear blue, conveying a sense of distance which is both calming and reassuring. They blend with muted pinks and reds to resemble well-worn, slightly faded damasks. In many respects these colours are the familiar mainstay of the garden, in possession of an unassuming elegance, and against which more powerful, more suggestive schemes may be set.

Underlying this apparently simple scheme is a deep understanding of the use of colour. Here Universal pansies, 'True Blue', are casually placed amongst random drifts of the colourful daisy, *Bellis* 'Medicis', to create an arresting yet utterly pleasing combination.

Success is in no small measure due to a matching of the dash of egg-yolk yellow which appears in both flowers.

A lovely companion planting such as this is not difficult to achieve. Here the violet-blue flowers of *Campanula lactiflora* tone with the rounded magenta-pink blooms of the old fashioned Gallica rose, *Rosa* 'Président de Sèze'.

Dramatic purple flowers of *Stachys macrantha* 'Robusta' harmonize splendidly well with the violet-blue bells of *Campanula lactiflora* 'Telham Beauty'. Creative plantings, as this one, carried out with confidence serve to lift a garden border out of the ordinary.

Violet-crimson flowers of the rambling rose, *Rosa* 'Bleu Magenta', pick up the coloured veining of the hardy geranium which grows at its feet. An arrangement like this one is simple but yet very effective.

Spectacular colour combinations may be had by utilizing clematis to climb over shrubs, up into trees or to weave through flower borders. In this instance *Rosa gallica officinalis*, the red rose of Lancaster, plays host to *Clematis integrifolia*.

An imaginative and highly successful partnering of two clematis. Velvet-red blooms of *Clematis viticella* 'Madame Julia Correvon' are teamed here with the dark lavender flowers of *Clematis viticella* 'Venosa Violacea'. Both flower in late summer.

The magenta flowers of the rose campion, *Lychnis coronaria*, are set against the purple spikes of a summer-flowering buddleja. An unusual combination which works extraordinarily well.

A well planned composition for the early summer which makes effective use of bold plantings of pale pink roses and hardy geraniums. Plant varieties have been deliberately kept to a few, and all within a colour range, in the belief, rightly, that simplicity often brings the greatest rewards. Here the end result is pleasing and lacking in any fussiness.

There is something of the cottage garden about this random grouping of violas and lamium in soft shades of pink, mauve and lavender placed together at the front of an herbaceous border.

Lovely to the eye and easy to achieve. Sugared-almond pink *Clematis montana* 'Tetrarose' climbs its way through the long racemes of *Wisteria floribunda* during the late spring.

Deep claret coloured orach, *Atriplex hortensis* var. *rubra*, is a foil in this setting to the pale pink cranesbill which surrounds it. Also included is a little, self-seeding viola.

A charming arrangement of *Geranium cinerum* 'Ballerina', a lavender, cream and white viola and one of the summer-flowering diascias. Colours such as these are always appealing to the eye.

Massed Colour

Just sometimes it is fun to go overboard with colour, to mass plants in such a way as to be sensational in terms of vibrancy and effect. Almost any colour in sufficient quantity will achieve a remarkable, often memorable, result and when two or three different ones are combined together, then the outcome will, almost certainly, be dramatic. Massed schemes, perhaps because they bring to mind municipal parks and gardens, are somehow associated with bright, occasionally vulgar, effects. This need not be the case, and whilst brilliancy is to be embraced in the right situation, quieter plantings should not be overlooked. When massing any kind of colour, be bold and decisive. Skimping on plants will result in an arrangement that looks thin, half-hearted and lacking in confidence. Too many colours will suggest uncertainty and will be in danger of losing direction. Remember, it is most often the simplest of ideas that work the best.

Bulbs are, of course, a particularly good way to achieve a massed display. Planted deeply they should reappear year after year so are, in a way, effective in terms of cost and labour. Where change is required, then they may be interplanted with something different at the start of each new season.

Ribbons of colour make for a different way of displaying spring favourites. Here the main components are tulips, *Tulipa* 'Golden Melody', wallflowers, 'Scarlet Bedding' and Universal pansies. When considering bedding schemes, always first decide whether you wish it to be arranged formally or naturally. In this situation the formal approach has been taken to achieve these results. Of course, once these are over they must be cleared away to make room for summer plantings.

Bulbs, in this case vivid red tulips, have been set in such a way as to thrust their way through other spring bedding. Here buttery-yellow wallflowers, which must be set out in the previous autumn, contrast with the tulip flowers. To achieve a similar effect, make certain that the colours you are using do, in fact, complement each other. Failure to do so may well result in something which is less than pleasing.

A simple, understated and yet dramatic use of tulips which are allowed to drift, almost as if by accident, through this border. The underplanting of forget-me-nots, with their starry, blue flowers, lifts the deep colour of the bulbs and gives to the whole scheme a lightness and airiness. Another planting, making use of the same colour but in very different shades, would be to combine the spikes of grape hyacinth, *Muscari armeniacum*, with the flowers of the forget-me-not.

When massing colours it is always advisable to place together those which will complement each other. This somewhat eclectic mix of rock roses, cranesbill and pansies are, in fact, in harmony.

Old-fashioned favourites, such as pansies and the hardy geraniums, when placed together really do give a feeling of an old cottage garden. Here pastel pink and violet-blue recall an impressionist painting.

Had these hardy geraniums and helianthemums been planted singly, then little if any lasting impression would have been made. As it is, planted in the company of others, the overall effect is of one body of colour gradually fading into, and being replaced, by another. In this way they draw attention to themselves, meriting a moment's pause and reflection.

Spires of *Verbena bonariensis* soar over deep pink *Salvia viridis* to give an unexpected treat to the eye. Mixing tall plants with shorter ones is never easy, but the results here are entirely satisfactory.

Annual marguerites and fuchsias unite here to make an attractive and striking display which should, with care, be long lasting. To promote flowers, deadhead both plants on a regular basis.

Roses and peonies, two of the most splendid of all garden plants, convey a very real sense of luxury to any border. Together they give a wonderfully rich display in early summer, their various colours blending together in near perfect harmony. Later, once these flowers are over, asters could be used to take their place. These too are excellent plants to mass together and are easy in cultivation.

Colour in the Border

Borders without colour would, it has to be admitted, be rather dull. After all, one of the principal delights of gardening has to be the arrangement of harmonious living pictures which will give satisfaction and be pleasing to the eye for as long a period as possible. That said, the organization of colour is not always as straightforward as might at first appear, and the path to achieving perfect results is certainly not an easy one. Plants, as we all know only too well, are fickle. Invariably they fail to grow exactly as expected, either growing too tall, failing to reach their expected height or, most likely, proving reluctant to flower at the very moment that is absolutely essential to the whole border composition.

Such pitfalls are not easily overcome and much will depend on trial and error, learning to work with your conditions, knowing your plants, resolving mistakes and building on successes. Do, though, be prepared to learn from others. Closely observe borders in other gardens, and there are now countless gardens open to the public, and note down combinations which especially appeal, and those which do not, the arrangement of plant material, mix of shrubs, perennials and annuals, means of staking, in fact anything which contributes to the overall effect.

Limiting the colour range is often one way of bringing about a pleasing result. Borders which encompass the whole colour spectrum can appear muddled and confusing. That is not to say your borders have to be of a single colour. Rather, select plants which will flower within a controlled range, perhaps employing a variety of shades and tints which are based on two or three main colours.

Rose, pink, magenta, a touch of violet, bronze, these colours, all within the same range, contribute a sense of unity to this mainly herbaceous border. The inclusion of some white and silver serves to break any degree of monotony as well as leading the eye onwards. Positioning the border along the length of a gravel path allows plants to spill over in an informal, random manner helping to avoid a contrived look.

A huge yew buttress makes a splendid background to this border which comprises summer perennials in shades of red, pink and a hint of lavender-blue. In the centre a white dahlia lifts the heart of the border.

This hot border of midsummer concentrates for its impact on red, orange and yellow. Purple-leafed foliage at either end of the border not only acts as a foil but also serves to create a sense of balance.

White achillea is used here at intervals to punctuate this border of deep pink, mauve and purple. Much thought has been given to the grouping of the plants to produce a gently undulating effect.

Placing plants closely together, so that they support each other, minimizes the need for other means of staking.

Backed by a grey stone wall and fronted by a flagged path, this border is beautifully planted with summer-flowering perennials. Note the way in which *Gladiolus communis byzantinus* has been placed as a ribbon of colour.

An alluring scheme for the early part of summer which makes excellent use of soft yellow, found in the lupins and irises, and white. A touch of silver is hinted at in foliage carried throughout the border.

Plants in profusion in complementary colours are the mark of this border seen at the start of summer. Designed for seasonal interest, there is much yet to flower. Natural larch poles support climbing roses.

Midsummer, and this border is possibly seen at its best, yet with the promise of more to come. Purple headed alliums, heleniums, phlox and coreopsis are all planted in generous clumps to give a well furnished look. Care has been taken to avoid an over-orchestrated appearance by placing taller growing plants towards the front rather than confining them to the back.

Pictured in late summer, this section of a larger border is principally planted in shades of lavender-mauve, deep pink and purple using asters, cone flowers (*Echinacea purpurea*) and *Verbena bonariensis* through whose tall stems may be glimpsed the butter-yellow flowers of *Rudbeckia fulgida* 'Goldsturm'. All of these perennials are long flowering to provide colour for many weeks from midsummer through into autumn.

Autumn Colours

The dying days of the gardening year produce some of its richest colouring. With certain plants this is their greatest season, but there are also many which reward with a final display after earning their keep in spring and summer.

Autumn Foliage

Any sadness that may be felt at the dying of the year, and it is a time for mixed emotions for the gardener, is, whatever, diluted with a sense of wonder at the sheer brilliance of the autumn colour which fills forest, woodland and garden alike. Few, if any, cannot be moved at the sight of a lowering sun streaming through a canopy of burnished leaves turned copper, gold and flame as the season draws to a close. At such a time a visit to a public arboretum, or even a drive down country lanes, becomes a magical and memorable experience. This is autumn at its best.

Autumn colour on a grand scale is much more difficult to achieve in a garden setting and, never more so, where space is restricted. But this does not mean that spectacular effects cannot be achieved even if they have to be in a more modest way. By choosing trees and shrubs with care, and selecting those which will perform well in other seasons too, it is perfectly possible to bring to the smallest of gardens much of the drama which is so typical of this time of year. Among those to consider are birches, cherries, maples, rowans, sumachs and whitebeams as well as colourful dogwoods and the spindle berries. Placed at intervals through the garden, the eye will be drawn from one set of colour to another.

What of course cannot be ignored is the difficulty of managing late colour in the garden. As the year progresses, and the autumn hues gather force, so summer colour is becoming fast spent and it is too often against a background of dead and decaying perennials that these flashes of brilliance and glory are to be enjoyed. Try, therefore, to position your end-of-season display in such a way as it may be viewed without other distractions. If this is not totally possible, then a little timely cutting back and clearing will help matters considerably.

Pseudolarix amabilis For beauty and hardiness, and where space is not a problem, grow the golden larch. As autumn approaches so leaves, growing in clusters, turn a vibrant, sunset yellow and are accompanied by cones, resembling pale green artichokes, which ripen to reddish brown. Planted in fertile, well drained soil in which there is an absence of chalk, this tree will mature into a remarkable, weeping specimen. 18 × 18m/52 × 52ft

Betula pendula Silver birch, by which name it is most commonly known, is valued as a small, spreading, delicately branched tree which is suitable for sunny or shady conditions. Spring catkins and shimmering yellow autumn foliage make this a tree for all seasons. 10 × 7.5m/ 33 × 25ft

Enjoy the papery white trunks of these trees placed together in a small grove. As the trees develop, so the white intensifies. Unfortunately birches are shallow rooted and dislike under-planting.

Acer campestre Showers of yellow coppery foliage herald autumn for this wonderful field maple. Occasionally flushed with red, the clear yellow leaves brighten any dull day at the end of the gardening year. Easy to grow, and very hardy, this acer is best reserved for the wild or woodland garden. In a more restricted, or formal area, select one of many smaller growing varieties offered by specialist nurseries. 10 × 8m/33 × 26ft

Larix decidua Gradually developing a drooping habit as it ages, the common larch is of conical habit when young. Dull gold autumn colour replaces fresh, light green leaves of spring. A vigorous, deciduous tree it is suitable for most soils except very wet or dry, shallow chalk. Generally speaking, larch is a woodland tree making it inappropriate for a normal garden. However, it is attractive and may be planted with a view to its removal when it exceeds its allotted space. 20 × 15m/66 × 49ft

Sorbus alnifolia Dense, purplish-brown branches carry heavily veined burnt copper leaves at the close of the season. Easily cultivated in any well drained, normal garden soil. Look out for small red fruits. 10 × 10m/33 × 33ft

Nyssa sylvatica The attractive, slow growing Tupelo has spectacular autumn foliage. Flashed red, gold and green this tree's leaves make an amazing contrast with dull, end-of-year skies. For a sunny spot in moist soil. 16 × 12m/ 52 × 39ft

Cercidiphyllum japonicum An elegant, autumn-colouring tree on which bright green leaves turn to droplets of shining yellow which, surprisingly, smell strongly of burnt sugar. The wondrous seasonal display more than compensates for insignificant flowers earlier on. 15 × 12m/ 49 × 39ft

Acer japonicum '**Vitifolium**' This large shrub, from the Japanese maple family, has significant, fan-shaped leaves which turn to rich colours in the autumn. An excellent garden subject for leaf shape and elegance of growth. 4.5 × 4.5m/15 × 15ft

Acer obtusatum An attractively shaped maple whose leaves turn a fiery red in the later part of the year. As may be seen from this illustration, this tree makes an excellent specimen. 15 × 5m/49 × 16ft

Liquidamber styraciflua Volcanic red and purple autumn foliage makes a dramatic impact in any situation where there is sufficient space to accommodate this magnificent tree. Unsuitable for shallow chalk, liquidamber prefers moist, well drained soil. 16 × 8m/52 × 26ft

Acer palmatum atropurpureum One of the most beautiful of maples and ideally suited to garden cultivation. Finely cut leaves and graceful arching stems contribute elegance and lightness and never appear out of place. 4.5 × 4.5m/ 15 × 15ft

Associate plantings in the garden are always important and need constantly to be borne in mind. Here the majestic plumes of the pampas grass are glimpsed through a canopy of red.

Prunus × *yedoensis* **'Yoshino'** The spreading branches of the Yoshino Cherry carry a profusion of almond-scented, bluish-white flowers in the early spring to be followed by bronze-orange foliage at the year's end. A fine, medium sized tree which is easy in cultivation in any soil which does not become water-logged. Pictured here in spacious surroundings, this prunus fits comfortably into the average garden and deserves to be more widely planted. 8 × 8m/ 26 × 26ft

Acer palmatum **'Senkaki'** The Coral Bark Maple is so named because of its conspicuous coral-red branches which are particularly effective in winter. Acid yellow-green autumn foliage is strikingly different from many other shrubs noted for their end-of-season colour. 4.5 × 4.5m/15 × 15ft

Acer palmatum All the cultivars of the Japanese maple are noteworthy for their elegant growth and outstanding autumn colour. Bright green young leaves of this variety turn rich ruby-red as the season progresses. Shelter from cold winds is desirable. 4.5 × 4.5m/15 × 15ft

Sorbus sargentiana Of rigidly branched habit, this rowan with red leaf stalks colours vividly in autumn. The crimson-red colouring produced is of velvet quality, topped by large rounded heads of small scarlet fruits. Sticky crimson buds remain throughout the winter to continue the colourful performance from this remarkable tree. Positioned somewhere on the boundary of the garden, it would make a wonderful backdrop to end-of-year plantings. 8 × 8m/26 × 26ft

Enkianthus perulatus Probably the best species for a small garden, this is a dense shrub of branching habit. Urn-shaped, white flowers are freely borne in spring, but it is the spectacular, burnt-scarlet autumn colour which makes this such a desirable plant for the garden. However, whilst tolerating some shade, therefore making it most suitable for a woodland situation, enkianthus is a lime-hater and must be grown on neutral or acidic soil. 3 × 3m/10 × 10ft

Disanthus cercidifolius Few shrubs can rival this excellent specimen for its range of autumn colours. Ruby-claret, papal purple, crimson and orange are all present and relatively long-lasting. Tiny purplish flowers at close of year complete the picture. An acid lover, this shrub should be planted in free-draining soil. Acquiring disanthus may present some problems as few general nurseries appear to offer it for sale. Seek out a specialist in the first instance. 3 × 3m/10 × 10ft

***Viburnum plicatum* 'Mariesii'** Wide-spreading, horizontal branches distinguish this most pleasing garden shrub which requires to be given sufficient space to show itself off to greatest effect. Huge white flowers produce an abundant spring display giving a 'wedding cake' appearance to the whole shrub. Oval, dull green serrated leaves gradually turn to faded burgundy giving a subdued but deeply satisfying autumnal effect. Easy in cultivation. 3 × 3m/10 × 10ft

Euonymus alatus Dull, bronzy-green leaves gradually turn to a riot of fire-flame reds as autumn gathers pace on this slow growing shrub. Showy fruits complete the display. Suitable for most soils, euonymus is not unhappy on chalk. 3 × 3m/10 × 10ft

Viburnum recognitum Viburnums offer such a wide variety of growing habits and ease of cultivation that they rightly deserve a place in any garden. This unusual variety has particularly glowing yellow foliage at the turn of the year. 3 × 3m/10 × 10ft

Rhus typhina The staghorn sumach is renowned for its interesting, architectural shape as well as for its brilliant colour at the close of the year. Its foliage embraces all autumn tints and often heralds the beginning of this season before other shrubs. Long after the leaves have fallen, erect seed heads continue through the winter gradually turning to dark brown. Take care, sumachs have a suckering habit and may, in some instances, become a nuisance. 5 × 6m/ 16 × 20ft

Fothergilla major A two season shrub. Enjoy fragrant white flowers in the spring and then, later in the year, the most brilliant of autumn colour. At this time foliage becomes a vibrant lacquer-red which is both impressive and long lasting. Slow growing, fothergilla is best planted in moist, acidic soil. In a small garden it would be an ideal subject around which to centre a border for an end of season display. 3 × 3m/10 × 10ft

Cercis canadensis 'Forest Pansy' A remarkable, slow growing form which only after several years will achieve tree-like proportions. Lustrous, rounded leaves turn a deep rosewood, a colour which is retained throughout the season. 10 × 10m/33 × 33ft

Rosa rugosa 'Alba' Rugosa roses colour well in autumn at which time they carry deep scarlet heps. The butter-yellow foliage is in marked contrast to the more common flame-reds of this particular time. 1.5 × 1.5m/5 × 5ft

Parthenocissus quinquefolia Of all climbers, this is surely one of the most oustanding for autumn colour. The true Virginia creeper, self-clinging, is capable of covering an entire house with its deeply cut leaves which slowly redden as the year advances. For a different effect, plant to grow through a tree, such as a mature apple, where it will cascade in ribbons. 12m/39ft

Cotoneaster horizontalis It is not inaccurate to describe the growth of this shrub as similar in appearance to a fishbone on account of its branching habit. The tiny leaves slowly colour with the approach of autumn and remain until winter has truly set in. Throughout the period small red berries add further decoration, unless raided by the birds. If required, it is perfectly possible to train this particular form against a wall. 2 × 2m/6 × 6ft

---

CONSIDER ALSO:

TREES:
Amelanchier 'Ballerina'
Crataegus × _prunifolia_
Rhus glabra 'Laciniata'

Cotinus coggygria 'Royal Purple'
Euonymus europaeus 'Red Cascade'

SHRUBS:
Acer palmatum 'Heptalobum Osakazuki'

CLIMBERS:
Parthenocissus henryana
Vitis coignetiae
Vitis vinifera 'Brandt'

Berberis thunbergii 'Atropurpurea' As winter approaches the reddish-purple foliage of this compact shrub intensifies in colour and is decked with long-lasting scarlet berries. Valuable for ease of cultivation and tolerance of a wide variety of growing conditions. 2 × 2m/6 × 6ft

Fruits and Berries

Showy fruits and berries are, in the main, one of the delights of autumn. Appearing at the same time as brilliantly coloured leaves, they add an additional sparkle and interest to trees and shrubs in the closing days of the year. But whereas fading foliage, however magnificent, is representative of decay and, of course, death, seasonal fruits are the culmination of nature's cycle and are a symbol of ripeness and richness.

Clinging on, as they so often do, into the depths of winter, until ravaged by hungry birds, fruits and berries take on a new lease of life when masked in hoar frost or lightly dusted with a coating of fresh snow. Then they become an exciting and integral part of a winter landscape which, in its own way, is as varied and interesting as that which is enjoyed during the long days of summer. Furthermore, gathered and brought into the house, they make for dramatic arrangements when placed in vases alongside dark, evergreen leaves and many coloured twigs.

As with all autumn tints, these riches of nature, because of their comparative brevity, have to be managed with care. Fleeting colours are much more difficult to place. In some seasons they may arrive early, stealing up to clash with a late summer scheme. In other years they may be dashed to pieces by the onset of early storms and gales. To allow for these possible eventualities, try to site fruiting trees and shrubs in such a way as they will enhance, rather than detract from, the overall garden scene.

***Cotoneaster frigidus* 'Cornubia'** Possibly too large for the smaller garden, unless employed as a screen at the back of a border, this hybrid is noted for its long, spreading branches from which hang many clusters of scarlet berries making for a spectacular autumn show. It is possible to train growth to a single stem to form a good small tree. Where cream and yellow fruits are preferred, then grow the form *Cotoneaster frigidus* 'Fructu Luteo'. 7 × 7m/23 × 23ft

Viburnum opulus **'Xanthocarpum'** Early autumn berries ripen on this deciduous shrub to a warm, butter-yellow. Later, as the year draws to a close, they change to become translucent. In the first part of the year train a clematis over the close growing branches. 4.5 × 4.5m/15 × 15ft

Malus × *zumi* **'Golden Hornet'** From late summer well into winter golden yellow crabs crowd this small tree making it most suitable as the centrepiece of an end-of-season, hot border. 4 × 6m/13 × 20ft

Sorbus **'Joseph Rock'** Hanging amongst prettily coloured leaves are to be found these yellow berries which follow flowers appearing earlier in the year. Mountain ashes are easily accommodated in garden situations. 12 × 7m/ 39 × 23ft

Cotoneaster salicifolius **'Exburyensis'** This graceful shrub carries these rather striking yellow berries in the later part of the year. An excellent, evergreen shrub which is well worth seeking out. 5 × 5m/16 × 16ft

Sorbus vilmorinii Leaves of this graceful, small tree turn to flame in the autumn. After the flowers these lovely, pale pink berries appear. Vilmorinii is most suitable as a specimen tree for the small garden. 5 × 5m/16 × 16ft

Sorbus cashmiriana 'Rosiness' A most decorative small tree which may, if the leader is pinched out, be grown as a spreading shrub. Berries, the size of marbles, are particularly noticeable after the leaves have fallen. 5 × 5m/16 × 16ft

Sorbus sargentiana These crimson berries of late summer, tightly packed in bunches, provide rich colour which is particularly conspicuous against tapering leaves of dark green. Superb amber and red autumnal tints. 5 × 5m/ 16 × 16ft

Sorbus 'Winter Cheer' Hanging in generous trusses, the berries of this mountain ash really do make a valid contribution to the dull days of winter and will, if not robbed by plundering birds, last for a lengthy period. 12 × 7m/39 × 23ft

***Malus × robusta* 'Red Sentinel'** As the leaves of this small growing crab fall, so these rosy-red apples are revealed which, in most years, are ignored by the birds at least until the onset of the worst of winter. 4 × 6m/13 × 20ft

The advantage of the smaller growing crab trees is that they can be fitted into even quite tiny gardens where they provide height, which is in scale, as well as seasonal interest.

Viburnum betulifolium Creamy-white flowers of summer pale into insignificance when compared with the lustrous, scarlet berries of autumn which hang in generous bunches from lofty, arching branches. 4.5 × 4.5m/15 × 15ft

Viburnum opulus The guelder rose continues in popularity on account of its white flowers of early summer, crimson autumn colour and translucent scarlet berries which appear in late season as glowing rubies. 4.5 × 4.5m/15 × 15ft

***Rosa moyesii* 'Geranium'** Blood-red flowers of the early summer are followed later on with these startling heps which decorate the long, arching stems throughout the autumn. Although this rose may be severely pruned in winter, it naturally forms a large, spreading shrub so should, ideally, be afforded plenty of space in the garden to show it off to advantage. Bring the fruits indoors to add cheer to winter days. 2.4 × 2.2m/8 × 7ft

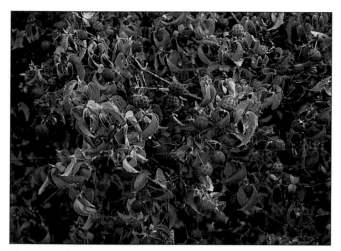

Cornus kousa The Chinese dogwood is an elegant shrub which is particularly attractive when covered in white flowers in summertime. Equally appealing are the strawberry-like fruits which deck the branches in autumn. 3.6 × 4m/12 × 13ft

Berberis thunbergii Pink foliage randomly splashed with white is the principal attraction of this compact berberis throughout the growing season. As autumn approaches stems are lined with tiny red berries. 1.2 × 1.2m/4 × 4ft

Of all berrying shrubs, pyracanthas, with their clusters of salmon, scarlet, orange and yellow berries, are amongst the most distinctive as autumn moves into winter. Bushes positively glow with these colours, bringing a warmth and sense of well-being to even the darkest of days. Wall-trained, they are able to lift and bring life to those sides of a house which attract little, if any, sun. For this alone they are well worth growing.

Arbutus unedo In maturity the Killarney strawberry tree develops a lovely, gnarled trunk although it is mainly grown for the fruits which appear alongside the cream, heart-shaped flowers. Preferring acidic soil, it will tolerate some lime. E, 5 × 5m/16 × 16ft

Photinia davidiana An attractive, evergreen shrub which bears bunches of juicy, succulent red berries in the later part of the year when they provide interest at a time when garden flowers are fast fading. E, 6 × 4m/20 × 13ft

Hypericum × inodorum 'Elstead' Bright yellow flowers shine through fresh, green foliage to be followed later by pretty scarlet-pink seed capsules. Unfortunately, these plants are prone to rust in most gardens. 1.2 × 1.2m/ 4 × 4ft

Euonymus europaeus Perfectly happy on chalk, the spindle tree is alight in autumn with leaves of the brightest scarlet together with shades of burnt copper. At this time berries of claret and deepest pink are to be seen hanging in generous bunches. A handsome tree to include in the mixed border or to grow as part of a shrub walk. A named variety to look out for is *Euonymus europaeus* 'Red Cascade'. 4.5 × 4.5m/15 × 15ft

Euonymus cornutus var. quinquecornutus Evergreen in mild areas, this splendid shrub with its unusually narrow, grass-like leaves is adorned in autumn with extraordinary berries which give the appearance of being suspended from crowns of pearl. End-of-year foliage takes on a myriad of fiery tints, making yet another good reason for growing this particular euonymus. 2 × 2m/6 × 6ft

Callicarpa bodinieri* var. *geraldii At the year's end the leaves of this medium-sized shrub turn a deep purple and are followed by these remarkable berries which sparkle in the sunlight. 4 × 4m/13 × 13ft

Pernettya (Gaultheria) mucronata According to the particular clone, this small shrub will produce berries of white, pink, red, purple or black towards the end of summer and into autumn. Must be grown on acid soil. ○, E, 75cm × 1.2m/2.5 × 4ft

Of all garden shrubs, cotoneasters are hardy, quick-growing and easy in cultivation thriving on most fertile soils providing that they are fairly free draining. Although the flowers themselves are inclined for the most part to be insignificant, the sprays of berries, in shades of red, yellow, coral and black, which follow in the autumn, are highly prized by gardeners. Deciduous varieties seldom drop their leaves before putting on a fine show of autumnal tints.

***Arum italicum* 'Pictum'** As the rather strange, marbled leaves of this perennial disappear, so columns of orange berries are thrown up which, leafless, make a startling contribution to winter borders. ●, 25 × 20cm/10 × 8in

Iris foetidissima Watch out for the seed pods of the Gladwin iris to burst open in winter to reveal these brilliant seeds.It is in small ways such as this that the year is extended for the gardener. E, 45 × 60cm/1.5 × 2ft

Skimmia japonica Seasonal berries of a rich red bring the evergreen leaves of this easy shrub to life during the winter months. To effect pollination of skimmias, plant male and female varieties together. There is a so-called hermaphrodite cultivar, *Skimmia japonica* 'Veitchii'. *Skimmia japonica* 'Scarlet Queen', as its name suggests, may be relied upon to carry large trusses of red berries. All will succeed in partial or complete shade.

Bark and Stems

At their most striking in wintertime, trees, free of the distraction of leaf cover, make an exciting contribution to the garden scene. Etched against the sky, either at daybreak or as twilight gathers, they take on a majesty that is perhaps denied to them, or certainly is less apparent, at other times of the year.

In the first instance it is, of course, the colour of bark which is likely to be noticed. Even the most ordinary of trees are capable of making a very valuable statement in this way. But some, the star performers, are worth including in the garden almost for their bark alone. In these are to be found a richness of colour, pattern and textural quality which is particularly welcome out of season.

Acer griseum With folds of what looks like uncut paper peeling from the bark, it is of little surprise that this tree is commonly called the paperbark maple. Autumn leaves are a vibrant red and gold. 8 × 6m/26 × 20ft

Eucalyptus pauciflora **ssp.** *niphophila* Bark of this evergreen gum tree is wonderfully patterned green, grey and cream. Plant in a position to display this to advantage out of the reach of cold winds. ○, E, 10 × 8m/33 × 26ft

Cornus alba Grow this easy shrub for its vivid red stems which light up a winter border. No harm will come if this is hard pruned to ground level periodically. In so doing, new growth will be even brighter. 3 × 3m/10 × 10ft

***Salix alba vitellina* 'Britzensis'** Treat this shrubby willow to the same hard pruning as for Cornus alba to encourage brilliant scarlet and orange stems. Most spectacular when caught in the rays of a winter sun. 3 × 3m/10 × 10ft

***Cornus stolonifera* 'Flaviramea'** All through the winter the greenish-yellow stems of this dogwood contribute warm colour to the border. In summer small white flowers are produced, but these really lack any significance. Place towards the back of the border, or as part of a shrubbery, to come into its own as summer flowers peak and fade. May be hard pruned if required. Use in vases indoors where the massed stems can look most effective. 2 × 4m/6 × 12ft

Stuartia sinensis Peeling bark reveals creamy patches which, with the approach of autumn, darken to a brown-purple colour. Plant in a lightly shaded spot in moisture retentive soil which is rich in humus. 4.5 × 4.5m/15 × 15ft

Acer capillipes One of the snake bark maples noted for the white stripes which run down the bark, becoming more pronounced as the tree matures. New growth is of a coral colour. 10 × 8m/33 × 26ft

Prunus serrula Rich mahogany bark of this cherry appears polished by winter sunshine. A broad headed tree which is really grown for the splendour of its trunk. Place towards the back of a border. 9 × 9m/30 × 30ft

Betula ermanii Smooth, silky, grey bark looks as if it were a plaster mould. This is a medium sized tree for the border or as a lawn specimen when, in winter, its ghostly trunk will come into its own. 15 × 4.5m/49 × 15ft

Betula utilis* var. *jacquemontii The shimmering, silver, papery trunk of this fine specimen tree stands out even when cloaked in leaves. Two or three placed together would form an attractive copse, suitable even for a comparatively small garden. In autumn foliage turns a wonderful, golden yellow, albeit for a fleeting moment. Surround in spring with early flowering bulbs like china-blue *Chionodoxa luciliae*, glory of the snow. 15 × 5m/ 49 × 16ft

Colour Around the Garden

Colour need not be restricted to beds and borders and their grand set-piece displays when warmer days arrive. There are many ways for a gardener to bring colour to other areas and to colder seasons.

Alpine and Rock Garden

For so many gardeners alpine and rock plants have a special appeal. They see these tiny miniatures as minute jewels, each with its own particular sparkle and, when set together, forming a glittering prize. Nor is such a description entirely fanciful. For these are treasures which are demanding of attention if they are to thrive.

Most alpine and rock plants require good drainage. They much prefer to be planted in a gritty medium through which water will readily run. For many, the worst of the winter weather is nothing to being water-logged or to having water, even ice, collecting around the crown. Many, but by no means all, enjoy the warmth of the sun, something to bear in mind when establishing a new rock garden.

A visit to an alpine nursery will give a good indication of just how many rock plants there are. Choose from minute columbines, like the violet–blue *Aquilegia bertolonii*, the tiniest campanula, *Campanula arvatica*, miniature pinks like *Dianthus* 'Inshriach Dazzler' or *Dianthus* 'La Bourboule', small spurge, *Euphorbia denticulata*, gaudy *Lewisia cotyledon* hybrids, penstemons suitable for the garden of a doll's house, *Penstemon pulchellus*, even a miniature cotton lavender, *Santolina elegans*. The list is endless and, ultimately, choice will reflect personal taste and will depend on the colour scheme which is being planned.

A colourful mixture of rock plants. In this garden the plan has clearly been to create a tapestry of colour rather than to consider a more limited, restricted scheme. Here are to be found a variety of rock roses, helianthemum, in shades of white, yellow, orange and red together with low growing, creeping cranesbill and lady's mantle, itself not technically a rock plant. A path allows for close inspection of the plants.

Fritillaria pyrenaica From the Pyrenees, and known as the Pyrenean snakeshead, this bulb produces these lovely flower heads of dusky purple, chequered with yellow, in the spring of each year. 30cm/1ft

As may be seen here, this fritillary is at its best when allowed to naturalize in grass. However, cutting should be delayed until the flower has had time to set and broadcast seed.

Pulsatilla vulgaris rubra Flowering at Easter, hence the name the Pasque flower, this is a long-lived perennial of a rich wine-red. Plant in a sunny position in soil which contains plenty of horticultural grit. 30 × 30cm/1 × 1ft

Pulsatilla vulgaris Normally deep purple, this particular form is of a pale lilac. Once the flowers are over they will be followed by wonderful, silky seedheads which, in turn, will produce a series of babies around the parent plant. 30 × 30cm/1 × 1ft

Sempervivums, or house leeks, make splendid subjects with which to fill containers especially in situations where they are likely to be neglected. These succulents will put up with a great deal, including little in the way of water in summer.

Erinus alpinus A delightful, short lived perennial alpine plant which may be relied upon to seed around gently. Pink flowers are produced in the early summer. Good for a crevice, as illustrated here. ○, E, 2.5–5cm/1–2in tall

Ajuga reptans '**Pink Surprise**' An extraordinarily pretty form of bugle with lilac-pink flowers as opposed to the more widely seen blue. Foliage is evergreen so most suitable as year-round ground cover. 15 × 60cm/6in × 2ft

Bright colours of spring. Everyone is familiar with the purple aubrieta and yellow alyssum, used in this instance to tumble over and clothe a low stone wall. Cut back hard once the flowering period is over.

Dianthus 'Gravetye Gem' Old-fashioned pinks are one of the delights of the garden in summer not only for their pretty flowers but also for their heavenly scent. Here is a tiny one which is ideally suited to the rock garden, for a trough or to fit snugly among other plants at the front of a border. Another choice of similar size would be Dianthus 'Waithman Beauty'. ○, E, 15 × 30cm/6in × 1ft

Lamium maculatum 'Wootton Pink' A form of dead nettle which is not at all invasive. On the contrary, this perennial is an excellent ground cover-plant and is delightful when covered with shell-pink flowers in summer. 15 × 30cm/6in × 1ft

Diascia cordata Flowers of this small perennial are produced throughout the summer and, if the weather is mild, well into autumn. An excellent subject for the rock garden. 20 × 20cm/8 × 8in

221

Herb and Kitchen Garden

All too often the herb and kitchen gardens are considered purely as functional and are, therefore, relegated to an out-of-the-way area only to be visited for the express purposes of gathering or tending crops. A legacy from the days of the grand country house, when the walled kitchen garden was usually sited at some distance from the house, this is a practice which deserves to be discontinued for both vegetables and herbs have a valuable contribution to make to colour in the garden.

True, it has to be said, in recent times there has been a revival of interest in creating formally designed herb gardens where the emphasis is firmly placed on pattern, colour and form rather than to serve any serious domestic purpose. Such gardens are highly decorative and much admired. In small gardens, where space is at a premium, then herbs are often included for their ornamental value and do, of course, sit easily with other herbaceous perennials in the mixed border.

The same cannot, sadly, be said of vegetables. In too many cases there is a reluctance to grow these other than for their primary purpose, to be eaten. The imaginative gardener will naturally recognize the merits of many vegetables and will wish to include them, not least for their colour, as part of general border schemes.

Summer flowering roses, which may be picked for the house, are central to this formally designed herb garden where sage, rosemary and chives, for kitchen use, are included with pansies and lavender grown for flower colour.

Lavender remains a firm favourite for both the herb garden as well as for the more general border. This French one, *Lavandula stoechas*, is combined here with a pale pink bistort, *Polygonum bistorta*.

This highly ornate corner of a garden demonstrates how, with decorative and imaginative planting, a working area can be integrated easily and successfully into an overall design. Vegetables with interesting leaves help to achieve this.

These tightly packed rows of chard, beetroot and lettuce have been interplanted with scarlet and orange nasturtiums for a contrast of colour. The red flowers exactly pick up the stems of the glossy beetroot leaves.

Combining traditional cottage garden plants works well where account is taken of colour harmony. Here the yellow evening primrose and dark mauve lavender are punctuated with the fresh green leaves of spearmint.

Traditional herb gardens, such as this fine example, more often than not are based on a formal design in which any paths are of brick or flag construction and beds, based on squares and rectangles, are divided one from another by low box hedging. Within these individual plots a single plant is cultivated. Well tended, and with hedges neatly clipped, these become exceedingly pleasing features in any garden. Recently herbs have been incorporated into the kitchen potager.

The onions contained within this box edged bed are arranged to be decorative until the point at which they are harvested. In contrast are the purple leaves of the viola which are allowed to smother any spare ground.

Wavy asparagus foliage, left to run to seed, provides an exciting variation in form and texture to the plump lettuces which grow at its feet. Both these crops are, of course, edible.

Runner beans, with their orange-red flowers, tied into a neat framework of string and poles, could well be sited at the back of a mixed border where they would not look at all out of place.

Using a mixture of colour and form can, when carried out successfully, bring about the kind of random planting which is so suggestive of the cottage garden of a past era. Here chives and mint jostle with each other for attention.

The Water Garden

You may, if you are very fortunate indeed, be in the enviable position of having natural water, in the form of a stream or a pond, within your garden. Most people, though, have to rely on something which is artificially created and whilst this in itself is not a problem, disguising the installation often is. All too often it is possible to end up with an uncoordinated arrangement of plants which, at best, provide haphazard colour through the year and, at worst, become a confused and tangled mass. Planning the water garden for colour effects requires the same attention to detail as other areas of the garden, with the added constraint of choosing those plants which will associate well with water and enjoy, in many instances, moisture retentive soil.

It may well be that the best policy is to select plants which will perform well together in a particular season, say spring, and accept that this is the time of year when the water garden will be at its best. For the rest of the year the emphasis will be on maintaining a tidy appearance with, perhaps, the inclusion of a massed, block planting of a single perennial to give flower colour at another time. Planning colour in this way will, except when working on a large scale, give very much more satisfying results.

These candelabra primula, in shades of orange, purple and red, have been planted in such a way as to make a statement of colour which is both intentional and uncompromising. Contrast is brought about with yellow flag irises and golden sedge, the whole being planned for the early summer. Any later flowers will be considered secondary to this main show. Large, paddle leaves of lysichiton provide variety of form.

Primula sieboldii Shades of palest pink, mauve and white give a delicacy to this variety of primula which flowers in the spring in a cool, moist situation. Mark the spot for by midsummer it will have died down completely.
15 × 15cm/6 × 6in

Visit a specialist nursery to discover countless varieties of primula to bring colour to the water garden from early spring until midsummer.

Primula pulverulenta A splendidly dark form of candelabra primula, the name deriving from the way in which the flowers are arranged in tiers around the central stem. Enjoy this one in early summer. 60 × 30cm/2 × 1ft

Of all aquatic plants, that is to say those which grow in water, water lilies remain an all time favourite. Whatever the size of your pond, you will find something to suit you both in terms of spread and colour.

***Caltha palustris* 'Flore Pleno'** Bring a splash of spring colour to the pond's edge with this double form of perennial marsh marigold. Clump forming, it enjoys moist soil in a sunny, open situation. 30 × 30cm/1 × 1ft

Primula florindae Deliciously scented, citrus–yellow bells appear during summer for several weeks at a time. Plant this perennial in a spot where it will receive some shade during the day. 75 × 75cm/2.5 × 2.5ft

Lysichiton americanus These extraordinary spathes appear in the spring before the huge leaves develop. Skunk cabbages will in time colonize a damp area and may be raised from seed although it will take some years for a plant to flower. 1m × 75cm/3 × 2.5ft

Lysichiton camtschatcensis A white form of skunk cabbage which is slightly smaller in habit. Most spectacular at the start of the year when planted in clumps in the margins of a stream or pond. 75 × 60cm/2.5 × 2ft

Geum rivale **'Leonard's Variety'** Nodding heads of the perennial water avens look particularly attractive when placed beside a pool. This named form, flowering in spring, is well worth seeking out. Unfussy as to situation. 45 × 45cm/1.5 × 1.5ft

Astilbe **'Erica'** All of the summer-flowering astilbes carry these wonderful plume-like flowers over pretty cut-leafed foliage. This cultivar, which is perennial, is of a soft pink and is grown here against a dark red berberis. 1 × 1m/ 3 × 3ft

Mimulus **'Orange Glow'** Either you will warm to the glowing colours of this summer perennial, which is ideal for creating a hot effect, or you will feel that it requires just that little bit too much in the way of daring. Whatever, this is an unusual variety which will have to be acquired from a specialist nursery. All mimulus should be planted in moisture retentive soil for best results. 60 × 60cm/2 × 2ft

The Winter Garden

Winter is not, as everyone knows, a season of extravagant colour. For the vast majority of plants this is a time of rest before the familiar cycle starts once more. And yet it is not without interest. Trees and shrubs, laid bare, reveal their structure and form, vistas, which remain closed in summer, are opened to view and evergreens are etched more sharply against a steely sky.

But it is the flowers in the borders which attract most attention and which give so much pleasure. Perhaps it is because they are few and far between, the surfeit of summer long over, that they are particularly treasured. Or maybe it is the lift that they give to days which are so often gloomy and grey. Or there again, it may be recognition of their tenacity, their hold on life, growing against all the odds that winter can throw in their way.

Here are to be found the earliest of the bulbs – aconites, chionodoxa, crocuses, cyclamen, the first daffodils and, of course, snowdrops. To these may be added miniature irises and those most wonderful of early flowering perennials, hellebores. Among these, before the *Helleborus orientalis* forms, are those like the Christmas rose (*Helleborus niger*), red stemmed *Helleborus foetidus* 'Wester Flisk' and the beautiful *Helleborus lividus*. Add to this flowering shrubs, coloured conifers, and even a clematis or two, and the picture is very much alive.

Conifers and heathers are always considered by many to be one of the mainstays of the garden in winter. Here large evergreen and ruby coloured conifers have been planted with sweeps of winter-flowering heather, *Erica carnea*, in a broad island bed to give a vibrant display of colour. Equally attractive would be an architectural arrangement of stems, winter bark and berries placed at intervals throughout the garden.

Iris unguicularis Flowers of the lovely Algerian iris appear over dense grassy foliage in brief spells throughout the winter and early spring. Ideally, plant in poor soil against a hot, dry wall. E, 20 × 60cm/8in × 2ft

Cyclamen coum Allow hardy cyclamen to colonize in drifts underneath the canopy of deciduous trees for a brilliant splash of winter colour. All forms will repay close examination for the delicacy of the flower. 10cm/4in

***Iris reticulata* 'Harmony'** The china blue flowers of this early dwarf iris are a delight at this time of year. To increase stocks, propagate by division during the late summer. ❍, 10–15cm/4–6in

Galanthus nivalis Flowering at the start of the year, snowdrops really do act as heralds of what is to come. Position in some shade and divide the bulbils immediately the flowers have gone over and before the leaves wither. 15 × 15cm/6 × 6in

Eranthis hyemalis Enjoy the sunny yellow, goblet-like flowers of the winter aconite in late winter. Tubers will flourish in humus-rich soil in a semi-shaded situation. A most welcome addition to the garden. 10 × 15cm/4 × 6in

Jasminum nudiflorum The highly popular winter-flowering jasmine comes alive with butter-yellow flowers during the winter months. Widely grown, this is a shrub which may be trained against a wall or to cover a fence. 3m/10ft

Hamamelis mollis Include this shrub as a centrepiece to the winter border where its delicate flowers will give all the appearance of strands of golden silk. Deliciously fragrant, witch hazels are slow growing and will take many years before they fill their allotted space. Later in the year when the flowers are spent and the leaves fully developed, they may be used as a host plant for a climber such as a clematis. 2.4 × 3m/8 × 10ft

Clematis cirrhosa Encourage this early evergreen clematis to climb around a window where its small, bell–like flowers will deceive you into believing that spring has arrived. Afford it a sheltered spot. E, 2 × 1m/6 × 3ft

Narcissus bulbocodium Miniature daffodils may appear quite frail but provided that the bulbs are planted deeply, then these welcome cups of sunshine will flower year after year. Allow foliage to die down naturally. ◯, 15 × 20cm/ 6 × 8in

Helleborus lividus The deeply cut, glossy, veined leaves of this striking hellebore are attractive in their own right all year round. During the early months of the year they act as a foil to silky pink flowers which, if there are enough to spare, will last indoors in water for a number of weeks. Unfortunately, this is not the hardiest of hellebores and so should be given a sheltered position in which to thrive. E, ◑, 45 × 45cm/1.5 × 1.5ft

Colour in the Conservatory

Conservatories are once more fashionable. These glass additions to the house, so loved by the Victorians of a hundred years or more ago, are now for many an affordable item and a relatively economical means by which to gain an extra room. Heated throughout the winter, they not only provide a warm, comfortable spot in which to relax but, more importantly, a place in which to grow any number of exotic, colourful plants.

If you are fortunate enough to own a conservatory, or to have a greenhouse in the garden which you are able to keep free of frost, then you will be able to enjoy year-round colour, even at a time when there is little in flower outside. A visit to a good florist or garden centre should prove to be a most rewarding experience and you will doubtless find yourself spoilt for choice.

But a conservatory does not necessarily have to be entirely for decoration. Any heated space can be utilized as a home for tender perennials which will not overwinter outside or a space in which to keep cuttings of half-hardy favourites. Alternatively, a heated conservatory is an excellent place for raising plants from seed.

Do remember that all indoor plants require regular watering and feeding. This is particularly so during the summer months when, without adequate ventilation, temperatures can rise to a point where plants may be placed under considerable stress.

Jasminum polyanthum Of immense value in a cool conservatory, this loveliest of jasmines will flood a room with a wonderful fragrance from a mass of beautiful white flowers in late spring with further flushes later in the year. Grow in a pot but take care not to provide too much in the way of heat. This is a climber which might well survive in a sheltered spot in a warm, enclosed garden. ○, E, 5m/15ft

Anisodontea capensis Tender in all but the most favoured of gardens, this sub-shrub will flower all summer long, and throughout the winter too if kept under glass. Do not be afraid to cut back to encourage new growth. ○, 1 × 1m/ 3 × 3ft

***Brugmansia* (*Datura*)** Angel's trumpets are a spectacular sight when fully in flower during the summer. Suitable for containers, they are best kept free of frost during the winter months. They may, if desired, be cultivated as standards. 1.2 × 1m/4 × 3ft

Fuchsia With so many different half-hardy fuchsias to choose from, it is possible to tie in with almost any colour scheme. Grow them for their brilliant flower from early summer onwards.

Pelargonium Familiarly talked of as geraniums, these tender plants are used widely throughout the summer to brighten up patios and terraces, to fill hanging baskets or as bedding outside. This particular variety is *Pelargonium* 'Madame Layal'.

Thunbergia alata Commonly known as Black-eyed Susan, this is an easily grown climber for the conservatory or greenhouse which is usually in flower for the greater part of the summer. Try it outside in a very warm spot. ○, 2m/6ft

Euryops pectinatus A small shrub from the south-western Cape of South Africa which is smothered in tiny, but very striking, yellow daisy flowers. Not fully hardy so needs to be kept frost free. 60 × 60cm/2 × 2ft

Clivia miniata Dark, glossy, strap-like leaves surround these flowers of deep orange which are borne in clusters over a long period of time. In containers this makes a spectacular plant for the conservatory or, indeed, as a pot plant within the house. With all such plants, care should be taken to provide them with appropriate growing conditions with regard to soil type, food, light and water. 60 × 30cm/ 2 × 1ft

Nerium oleander A small, ornamental tree which is widely grown in the South of France. In colder climates it is best placed outside in the summer months and returned to the conservatory or cool greenhouse for the winter.
1.2 × 1m/4 × 3ft

Plumbago capensis Flowers of sky-blue will, under cool glass, virtually obliterate the foliage of this climbing shrub in the late summer and early autumn. Easy to grow, it will flower freely in the second year from seed. 2m/6ft

Cymbidium ruspex **'Ivory Queen'** Wonderfully exotic flowers which require to be grown in a frost-free environment. Cymbidium is an orchid which may be grown successfully as a potted plant. 60 × 30cm/2 × 1ft

Pots and Containers

So much of summer in the garden is associated with colour. This is the season of beautifully arranged borders in which herbaceous perennials are at their peak, of colourful annuals contributing an additional glow, of flowering shrubs and trees, all of which are set off, ideally, by well kept lawns, swept paths and raked gravel. To this may be added a wealth of colour and interest achieved through an imaginative use of pots and containers.

For those with very tiny or even no garden at all, pots are one way of creating colour in a small space. In larger gardens they may be used to enliven dull spots in borders, as eye-catchers to close vistas, as pointers around the garden, to draw attention to a particular area or simply as decorative ornament. In every situation they may be employed to mark an entrance, such as either side of a doorway or positioned on gate piers, to furnish a terrace, patio or outside sitting or eating area, to line a pathway as a means of introducing a note of formality, or merely in a functional manner as a way of growing half hardy plants which will require winter protection.

Whatever, it must be remembered that pots and containers, once filled with soil and planted out, are permanently in need of care and attention. They must not, first and foremost, be allowed to dry out. This may well mean watering as often as twice a day during very hot spells. They too will need feeding regularly throughout the season to maintain plants in a healthy condition. Finally, attention to deadheading will encourage repeat flowers and ensure that arrangements remain fresh and trim.

Displays of this kind can really only be effected with brightly coloured annuals which, if not fully hardy, may not be put outside until all danger of frost has passed. Here both boxes and baskets have been positively crammed with flower which, if routinely deadheaded, will give a succession of bloom right through the season until the cold weather sets in. Annuals may be used in a variety of ways. For best results, limit your range of colours and plant en masse.

Hanging baskets, like this one which is crowded with fuchsia, petunia and lobelia, would be splendid positioned by a back door to serve as an invitation into the garden proper. Plants here have been kept within a particular colour theme.

A gorgeous array of colour cleverly arranged in a single hanging basket. What may be seen from this is the importance of including sufficient plant material to guarantee a full and complete effect.

Cheerful bedding plants join hands with the more sombre, permanent ivy around this window to form an integrated summer display. The containers, a window box and a basket positioned on the wall, have been disguised, completely by the massed planting. The bright colours of the plants stand out strongly against the white wall and window.

This is a garage – totally obscured by pots and containers of varied greens, yellows and greys. Such a composition can be re-arranged in a moment as the mood takes you.

Setting these hot colours against a dark, evergreen background certainly shows them to advantage as well as assisting in containing them. All planted in pots, the blazing yellows and fiery reds lead the way to, and highlight, the front door.

The glowing, ember colours of these acers are well matched to the dark, terracotta pots which contain them. A plain green background serves to set them off and acts as a contrast of leaf shape.

Lifting herbaceous perennials from the traditional setting of a border and placing them in pots where both flower and foliage may be admired really does work. Here the foliage of the agapanthus is as important as the flower.

A formal setting lends itself to containers like this classical urn. Whether empty or, as in this garden, filled with spring tulips and complementary pansies, they never appear out of place. Colours have been deliberately restricted and, at this time of the year, chosen to tie in with and reflect the bracts of the tall euphorbia which is placed behind. The flagged path on which the urn is placed helps to secure the entire arrangement.

Orange and red, although an unusual combination, do, in fact, work together well. This handsome terracotta pot contains a fine specimen of *Fritillaria imperialis* surrounded by blood-red tulips. Once spring has gone it can be replanted.

These two Versailles planters contain box pyramids as permanent structure. In springtime a touch of colour is added with flowering tulips. These work particularly well in surroundings which are otherwise deliberately plain.

Pots where the flower colour is severely restricted require the most confidence to create and yet are often the most pleasing to look at. The setting in which they are to be placed needs to be considered with care.

A wonderful sense of understated theatre is evident here in the placing of these splendid parrot tulips against this chalky blue paintwork. The stripe of the tulip is picked out in the colour of the pansy flower.

The formality of the trellis fence arranged in a series of arches demands the kind of repeated planting which is shown here. The focal point of each planter is the central, half-standard box ball, which could equally be of pyramid shape, which is then surrounded by a cool scheme of whites, greys and fresh greens, the whole being kept totally simple. Even without the flower colour, this would work as well in winter.

Wonderfully simple yet highly imaginative. Huge box balls sit comfortably into these black painted planters to mark the approach, in the most stylish manner, to the entrance of this town house. Note how the box is repeated in the low hedge where the level changes.

Annual colour is added to these pots to surround perennial plantings. In time the shrubs will grow to fill the entire container and will then have to be replaced.

Shocking pinks, such as these, cry out to be noticed at this entrance. Relying in the main on two flowering plants which are supported with complementary foliage gives the entire arrangement a satisfying unity.

This collection of spring flowers grouped together in terracotta pots is a delightful way in which to end a short path. The evergreen backdrop gives the whites an additional brilliance.

Painting this classically shaped, cast iron urn a deep shade of blue-green gives it a new look. Planting, in keeping, is deliberately simple, the leaves of the succulent being chosen to pick up the colour of the paintwork.

An evergreen window box which combines simplicity with style. Flower is restricted to the skimmias with both the box and ivy retaining the same colour and shape all year. Ivy climbing the wall reflects that in the container.

Using different plants with flowers from the same colour spectrum can very often achieve a similar result to a scheme in which one particular variety of plant is used. Here all the pinks tie in together.

An old copper pot, splendidly planted, is placed in the middle of a crossing point of two paths, the intersection being marked with fine Irish yews. Surrounding plantings appear informal, even accidental, but are actually tightly controlled.

A charming mixture for the early spring gives the effect of a cottage garden in miniature. Colours are, though, chosen with care and limited to yellow, mauve and violet-blue.

Purples, reds, mauves, pinks, whites and a hint of yellow form a happy mixture in this pot collection which is sited on the treads of these shallow steps leading to an entrance.

245

Winnie the Witch and her big black cat
Wilbur were getting ready for a party.
It was a fancy dress party to celebrate
Cousin Cuthbert's birthday.

'What will we wear, Wilbur?' asked Winnie.
'We'll have to think about that.'

Winnie thought about it.

Cinderella?
No.

A bear?
No.

The Queen
of Hearts?
No, no!

Then Winnie had
a fantastic idea.

She waved her
magic wand,
shouted,
Abracadabra!

And there she was, wearing a pirate costume.
Wilbur was in a parrot suit.

Winnie was pleased.
'We look fantastic!' she said.

Wilbur was embarrassed.

'We look ridiculous,'
he thought.

Winnie jumped onto her broomstick,
Wilbur jumped onto her shoulder,
and they flew off to the party.

There were some wonderful
costumes at the party.

Fairies, clowns, a lion, a princess,
some spacemen and *lots* of pirates.

Happy Birthday, Cuthbert!

The other pirates admired Winnie's parrot.
Wilbur flapped his wings.

'All we need now is a treasure map,' one pirate said.
'I found a treasure map in my pocket,'
said another pirate.
'So all we need now is a ship.'

'I can do that,' said Winnie.
She waved her magic wand,
shouted,

Abracadabra!

And there was a pirate ship,
at the bottom of
Cuthbert's garden.

'Hurrah!'
shouted the pirates.
They climbed aboard
and sailed away.

'Yo-ho-ho!' shouted Winnie's pirates. 'Being a pirate is fun!'

They climbed up the masts.
They danced the hornpipe.
They walked the plank,
until Winnie fell in.

Luckily she could swim.

Wilbur climbed up to the crow's nest for a sleep,
but there was a crow inside.

'Caw!' said the crow.
She didn't want to share with a parrot.

Winnie's pirates got out the treasure map.
There were islands all around their ship.
Which one was the treasure island?

But then they saw an island
that looked exactly like the one
on the treasure map.

Winnie and her pirates splashed ashore.
They climbed to the top of a hill and
looked down.

There was another band of pirates digging up the treasure.
They had swords and daggers, cutlasses and blunderbusses.

They looked fierce.

'Will we stay and fight?' asked Winnie. 'Or go home?'

Winnie's pirates shouted . . .

'GO HOME!'

The real pirates looked up
and saw Winnie's pirates.

They ran back to their ship
with their swords and daggers,
their cutlasses and blunderbusses . . .

and sailed away.

Winnie's pirates were very surprised.

'Hurrah!' they shouted.
'We are fierce pirates!'

They ran down to the hole
in the sand and started digging.

It was hard work.

But at last they dug out the treasure chest.

Winnie lifted up the lid. The chest was empty.
'Shiver me timbers!' shouted Winnie's pirates.

'We've been hornswoggled!'

But Wilbur saw something
shining in the sand.

What was it?

He started to dig
and dig.

Out came a big shiny box.
And inside the box were lots
and lots of shiny tins . . . of sardines!

'Meee-yo-ho-ho!'
Wilbur was delighted. He loved sardines.

Winnie's pirates were not delighted.

But Winnie had a
wonderful idea.

She waved her wand,
shouted,
Abracadabra!

And the
treasure
chest was full
of shiny treasure.

Now Winnie's pirates
were delighted.
They carried the treasure
and Wilbur's sardines
back to the ship.

It was time to go home, but there was
no wind to blow their ship home again.

'I can fix that,' Winnie said.
She waved her magic wand,
and shouted, *Abracadabra!*

WHOOSH!
The pirate ship flew through the air.

PLOP!
It landed back at the party.

Winnie's pirates shared the treasure with Cousin Cuthbert and his friends. They were delighted, too.

Wilbur didn't share his sardines.

'Being a pirate is fun, Wilbur,' Winnie said. 'But being a witch is much more fun.'

'*Purr, purr, purr,*' said Wilbur.

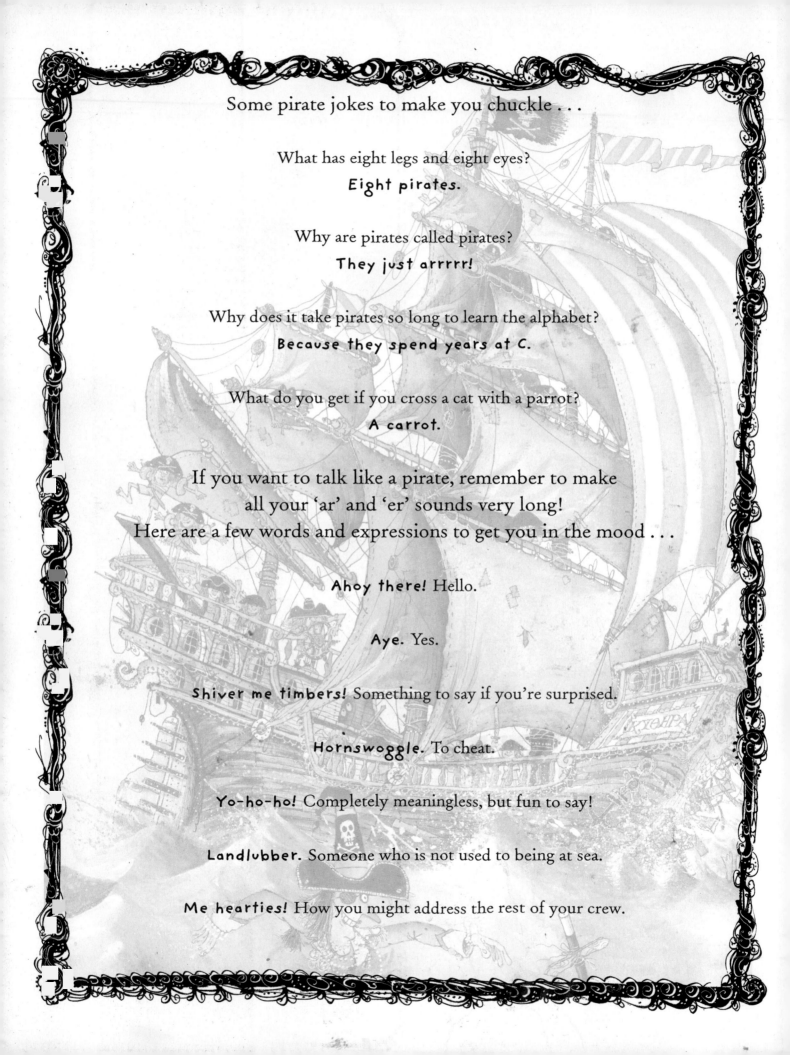

Some pirate jokes to make you chuckle . . .

What has eight legs and eight eyes?
Eight pirates.

Why are pirates called pirates?
They just arrrrr!

Why does it take pirates so long to learn the alphabet?
Because they spend years at C.

What do you get if you cross a cat with a parrot?
A carrot.

If you want to talk like a pirate, remember to make
all your 'ar' and 'er' sounds very long!
Here are a few words and expressions to get you in the mood . . .

Ahoy there! Hello.

Aye. Yes.

Shiver me timbers! Something to say if you're surprised.

Hornswoggle. To cheat.

Yo-ho-ho! Completely meaningless, but fun to say!

Landlubber. Someone who is not used to being at sea.

Me hearties! How you might address the rest of your crew.